The French Noel

Publications of the Early Music Institute

Thomas Binkley, General Editor

Accompaniment on Theorbo and Harpsichord: Denis Delair's Treatise of 1690.
A Translation with Commentary by Charlotte Mattax.

Thomas Binkley and Margit Frenk. *Spanish Romances of the Sixteenth Century.*

Michael Collver and Bruce Dickey. *A Catalog of Music for the Cornett.*

J. P. Freillon Poncein. *On Playing Oboe, Recorder, and Flageolet.*
Translated with an Introduction by Catherine Parsons Smith.

Luis Gásser. *Luis Milán on Sixteenth-Century Performance Practice.*

Robert A. Green. *The Hurdy-Gurdy in E̶̶̶* *rance.*

George Houle. *Molière's Comedy.*

George Houle. *tice.*

Sterling Scott J

Antoine Mahau *sverse Flute.*
Translated an

Ockeghem's Mis *Edited in all the Modes.*
With an Intro

Monsieur de Sa *t: With the Harpsichord,*
the Organ, an *ed by John S. Powell.*

David Hogan S

The French Noel

With an Anthology of 1725 Arranged for Flute Duet

Betty Bang Mather & Gail Gavin

INDIANA UNIVERSITY PRESS

Bloomington and Indianapolis

Library of Congress Cataloging-in-Publication Data

The French noel : with an anthology for two transverse flutes or other melody instruments / [edited by] Betty Bang Mather and Gail Gavin.
1 score. — (Publications of the Early Music Institute)
Performing ed. of 16 popular noels arr. for 2 flutes by (Jean-Jacques?) Rippert and published in the collection: Brunettes ou petits airs a II dessus (1725).
Includes facsimile, French words with 1st verse translations into English, and a lengthy introd. in English on noel history and interpretation.
Includes bibliographical references (p.   ) and index.
ISBN 0-253-21025-9
1. Flute music (Flutes (2)), Arranged—Scores.
2. Duets (Unspecified instruments (2)), Arranged—Scores.
3. Carols, French—Instrumental settings. 4. Christmas music.
I. Mather, Betty Bang. II. Gavin, Gail.
III. Rippert, Jean-Jacques. IV. Brunettes. V. Series.
M288.F82   1996   95-10193

Cover picture: Woodcut from title page of *La Grande bible des noels* (Troyes and Paris: Oudot, 1684). Courtesy of the Library of Congress.

Title page picture: Detail from Jean Christophe, *Baptême du dauphin, fils du Louis XIV* (Versailles Museum). Courtesy of the Réunion des Musées Nationaux, Paris.

CONTENTS

To those wishing to learn the true art of playing the little French airs.

PREFACE

From the Renaissance to the Baroque, French noels joined sacred texts with profane music and dance. To experience the many aspects of noels, readers of this book can play them, sing them, and dance to their music, as did French peasants, aristocrats, and members of the middle class during the 16th century.

In 1725 a "M.ʳ Rippert" published in Paris an anthology of popular tunes arranged for two flutes or other melody instruments. He called the volume:

Brunettes
ou
Petits Airs a II Dessus,
a l'usage de ceux qui veulent apprendre
a joüer de la Flûte-Traversiere.

Brunettes
or
little airs for two treble instruments,
for the use of those who wish to learn
to play the transverse flute.

The duets have been ascribed to the highly respected woodwind maker Jean-Jacques Rippert, who worked in Paris from before 1696 until after 1716, but they may instead have been fashioned by a younger member of the Rippert family.[1] The *Brunettes ou Petits Airs* of the anthology title are *chansons populaires* (simple melodies of the people). Often a shepherd and shepherdess sing of their love. Like the bucolic bagpipes, chalumeaux, and flutes to which the shepherds sang and danced, these traditional airs came much into fashion among the French aristocracy during the late 17th and early 18th centuries. Like the *chansons populaires,* the noels relate tales of shepherds and shepherdesses along with their particular stories of Mary and the Child. In fact, the melodies of most noels are borrowed from popular *chansons.* The 16 noels arranged by Rippert are among the most frequently published in the late Baroque, and many go back to the early Renaissance.

Part I of this book investigates the history of noels and all possible clues to their interpretation. Chapter 1 examines the meaning of the word *Noel,* the noels as sacred parody and rustic poetry, the relationship between noels and dance, the place of noels in the church, and the musical style in 18th-century noel settings. Chapter 2 explores the influence of Renaissance dance steps on purely vocal melodies, and of 17th-century bar lines, meter signs, and binary form on Renaissance song. Chapter 3 gives the known choreography for one noel and some possible steps for others. Chapter 4 discusses the performance of noel melodies, based chiefly on their lyrics, to show instrumentalists how to play the noels and similar pieces without given lyrics. Chapter 5 explores the long-standing relationship between flutes, shepherds, angels, and song.

Part II makes these charming pieces available in a performance edition that provides the noel texts. Rippert, through his titles, gives only the first line of the lyrics that he and others of his day presumably knew well. Today's players, unless supplied with the

---

1. William Waterhouse, *The New Langwill Index: A Dictionary of Musical Wind-Instrument Makers and Inventors* (London: Tony Bingham, 1993), s.v. "Jean-Jacques Rippert." In 1696 Jean-Jacques Rippert was called *maistre faiseur d'instruments à vent* (master maker of woodwind instruments) and *faiseur de flûtes* (maker of flutes). In 1701 Joseph Sauveur named him and Jean Hotteterre *les plus habiles facteurs de Paris* (the most skilled makers in Paris). Surviving instruments by Rippert include four recorders, a flute, and an oboe.

original lyrics, can only guess at the affect, tempo, phrasing, and performance of ornaments in each noel.

The cover of this book shows the woodcut from the title page of our chief source of lyrics, *La Grande bible des noels* (Troyes and Paris, 1684). Appendices 1 through 3 furnish facsimile copies of three of our chief musical sources. Appendix 4 gives the scansions and almost word-by-word English translations of the first stanzas of the noels, so that readers not familiar with French can better understand the basic phrasing of the melodies.

We are deeply indepted to pioneer Patricia M. Ranum for her inspiration and guidance in our understanding the scansion of French songs, how the lines of lyrics fit the musical measures, and how the lyrics influence and are reflected in the articulation, phrasing, and ornamentation of the music. She was kind enough to review several drafts of this manuscript and point us in the right direction on many matters. Any remaining errors on these subjects are our own.

Many thanks also to a pioneer in another field, Jane Bowers, who some twenty years ago encouraged one of us, Betty Bang Mather, to purchase an original copy of the Rippert anthology from a London rare book dealer. A few years later at an annual convention of the National Flute Association she presented pictorial and literary evidence of the early use of transverse flutes, and with Mather played some of the early music. She also made her photograph of the Christophe picture available for the title page of this book. Our gratitude also to a newcomer to this field of research, John Anderies, who reminded us that vocal music and especially the *petits airs* were almost certainly the chief music played in France on the new conical, one-keyed flute; who kindly supplied some of our primary sources for chapter 5; and who reviewed a draft of this chapter. Much gratitude to Helen Chadima, who made suggestions for chapter 3 on the dance; and to Roger Mather and Jama Stilwell, who reviewed several versions of the manuscript. Thanks also to Geoffrey Hope and Carla Zecher, who gave last-minute help on early French poetry.

Warm appreciation to The University of Iowa for the Undergraduate Scholar Assistantship that made it possible for one of us, Gail Gavin, to work on this book while completing her undergraduate studies. Thanks to Robert Sheldon and especially Carol Lynn Flanigan for their assistance in obtaining noel lyrics of the period from the Library of Congress, and to David Buch and again Patricia Ranum for help in obtaining lyrics from the Bibliothèque nationale of Paris. Finally, our gratitude to the Biblioteca Colombina of Seville, Spain; the Bibliothèque municipale of Lyon, France; the Bibliothèque de l'Arsenal and the Bibliothèque nationale of Paris, France; the Library of Congress; the Main Library and the Rita Benton Music Library of The University of Iowa; the Österreichische Nationalbibliothek of Vienna, Austria; and the Yale University Library.

Betty Bang Mather   Gail Gavin

Iowa City, Iowa
April 1, 1996

PART I

HISTORY AND INTERPRETATION OF NOELS

1

The Noel

From the late fifteenth century until the present day, noels have been sung happily by all classes of French men, women, and children in church and in their homes. The Christmas songs reflect the musical world in which they were composed, often using popular songs of the day for their melodies. The popularity and simplicity of noels was embraced by the masters of the French Baroque, many of whom arranged the tunes for keyboard or other instruments.

This book focuses on the 16 noels arranged for flute duet by Jean-Jacques Rippert or a younger member of the Rippert family in 1725. These songs represent a small corpus of the most popular noels, many of which originated in the Renaissance and later were repeatedly arranged by Baroque composers. Adrienne Fried Block's *The Early French Parody Noel*,[1] a study of Pierre Sergent's 16th-century *Grans noelz* collection (Paris, [1537?]), provided an excellent background for our study as well as a wide variety of primary quotes. Many of Rippert's noels are included in Sergent's collection.

The Meaning of *Noel*

The French word *noël* is believed to be related to newness, as in "good news" or "New Year."[2] Early uses of the word did not refer to Christmas or to songs sung at Christmastime; rather, *noël* was a cry to get attention or express joy. In Guillaume de Villeneuve's poem *Crieries de Paris* (end of the 13th century), a vegetable merchant announced his wares with the shout *Noël, noël* (News, news!):

Noël, noël, a moult grans cris.   Noel, noel, he cried in a loud voice.
J'ai raïs, de l'archault, raïs.[3]   I have roots, of the artichoke, roots.

Uses of the word *noël* to refer to the birthday of Christ occur from the 13th century onward.[4] By the late 15th and early 16th centuries, the word could also designate a song sung at Christmastime, as evidenced by the titles of collections of noel lyrics. By the 17th century, the word specified three kinds of Christmas tidings: the day of rejoicing itself; the songs that exulted in that news; and the exuberant cry at the birth of the Christ Child.[5] Antoine Furetière included these three usages in the *noel* entry of his *Dictionaire universel* (1690) and then reflected upon the former usage of the word:

NOEL. substantif masc. Fête de la Nativité de Nôtre-Seigneur. L'Advent de Noel *est le temps d'un mois, pendant lequel on attend la feste de* Noel, *et on se prepare à la celebrer.*

---

1. Adrienne Fried Block, *The Early French Parody Noël*, 2 vols. (Ann Arbor, Mich.: UMI Research Press, 1983).
2. Block, vol. 1, 7.
3. In Etienne Barbazan, ed., *Fabliaux et contes des poètes françois des XI, XII, XIII, XIV, et XVe siècles*, rev. M. Méon, vol. 2 (Paris: Crapelet, 1808), 282. Barbazan says that "noel" here means book of noels. Amédée Gastoué, *Le cantique populaire en France* (Lyon: Janin Frères, 1924), 114, disagrees. Block (vol. 1, 7) considers the two lines a public acclamation to call attention.
4. Emile Littré, *Dictionnaire de la langue française*, vol. 5 (Colombes: Gallimard et Hacette, 1957), 753. In Block, vol. 1, 8.
5. Block, vol. 1, 9.

NOEL, se dit aussi d'une chanson faite à l'honneur de Noel, *ou de quelque chose qui en depend.* Noel *nouveau. La grande Bible des* Noels.

NOEL, est aussi un cri de joye par lequel on témoigne souhaitter l'avenement du Messie.

On crioit autrefois Noel *en toutes sortes de fêtes et de réjoüissances publiques. Ainsi le peuples chanta* Noel *au Baptême de Charles VI et quand Charles VII fit son entrée dans Paris en 1437, et en autres occasions rapportées par Monstrelet, Alain Chartier, et dans la Chronique de Loüis XI remarquée par André du Chesne.*[6]

NOEL. masc. noun. Holiday of the Nativity of Our Lord. The Advent of *Noel* lasts one month, during which people await the feast day of *Noel* and prepare to celebrate it.

NOEL, this also means a song written in the honor of *Noel*, or something related to it. New *noel*. The great Bible [i.e., collection] of *Noels*.

NOEL, is also a cry of joy by which people show they hope for the coming of the Messiah.

Formerly, people cried *Noel* at all sorts of holidays and public rejoicings. Thus, the people sang *Noel* at the baptism of Charles VI and when Charles VII made his entrance into Paris in 1437, and on other occasions reported by Monstrelet, Alain Chartier, and in the Chronicle of Louis XI noted by Andre du Chesne.

Sources of Noel Texts

From the end of the 15th century, collections of lyrics called *noëls* began to appear. Some early manuscripts were elegantly written for wealthy households, but early printed collections were small, simple in format, and printed on cheap paper with numerous typographical errors. Sold unbound in the streets, they were clearly intended for use by common people.[7]

Noel collections often had long, descriptive titles. Many began with the designation *Bible des noelz* (Bible of Noels) first used by the Lyon printer Benoit Rigaud in 1554.[8] Collections usually were devoted solely to lyrics, though a few, such as *La fleur des noelz* (The Flower of Noels, attributed to the Lyon printer Jaques Moderne [1535]), included music for a few noels.

Most 17th- and 18th-century collections continued to provide either text or music, but we found only Christophe Ballard's *Chants des noëls* (Melodies of Noels, Paris, 1704; reprint 1712) to supply both. He gives music and text for only a few stanzas, referring readers for the rest to Nicolas Oudot's *Grande bible* publications and to a " M.ʳ Pellegrin."[9] Some authors printed and sold their own noel texts written to the melodies of familiar songs. The texts for two noels in our edition in Part II come from such 17th-century collections, one by François Colletet (*Noels nouveaux et cantiques spirituels*, Paris, 1665) and one by Pierre Binard (*Noëls ou cantiques nouveaux*, Troyes and Paris, 1678).

Noels were often identified by the first line of the song whose melody they borrowed (table 1). In many early collections, they are headed with the words *Noël sur* (Noel on) or simply *Sur* (On) followed by the name of the borrowed melody. Noel collections of the 17th and 18th centuries preserve the *Noël sur* designations, but most with music are named for the first line of noel lyrics. Rippert instead names Noel 14 for its drinking

---

6. Antoine Furetière, *Dictionaire universel, contenant generalement tous les mots françois tant vieux que modernes, et les termes de toutes les sciences et des arts*, vol. 2 (The Hague, 1690), 731. This work was written over a period of 40 years.

7. See Block, vol. 1, 17, and Douglas J. Rahn, "Melodic and Textual Types in French Monophonic Song ca. 1500," Ph.D. diss. (Columbia University, 1978), 58.

8. Frank Dobbins, "Noël," *The New Grove Dictionary*, vol. 13, 261.

9. "M.ʳ Pellegrin" was the Abbot Simon-Joseph Pellegrin. We do not know to which of Pellegrin's publications Ballard refers; all that we have seen give new noel texts for the old noel melodies.

song timbre, *Quand la Mer rouge apparut*. His Noel 2 is named for a song we could not locate, *Que de gentilles pelerines*. In our edition in Part II, we substitute a popular noel text to the same melody, *Quoi, ma voisine, és-tu fâchée?*. [10]

TABLE 1. Timbres and earliest known sources for noels in Rippert's *Brunettes ou petits airs a II dessus* (Paris, 1725).[11]

Noel Title and Author of Text if Known	Earliest Known Noel Source[12]	Noel Timbre and Type of Song if Known
1. *Où s'en vont ces gais bergers*	[first half of 17th c.]	*Où est-il mon bel ami allé, reviendra-t-il encore?* (timbre refrain)
2. *Quoi, ma voisine, és-tu fâchée,* by Pierre Binard	Binard, 1678	*Je me levai par un matin devant le jour*
3. *Laissez paître vos bêtes*	Arnoullet, c. 1517–67; or [Moderne], *La fleur* [1535]	None known
4. *Vous qui desirez sans fin*	*Noëls*, Paris, Arsenal MS 3176 (c. 1674)	*Magdelon, je t'aime bien*
5. *Chantons je vous prie*	c. 1520[13]	*Si le loup venoit*
6. *Tous les bourgeois de Châtre,* by Y.-L. Crestot	Sergent [1537?]	*Nous mismes a jouer* (theatrical chanson?)[14]
7. *Noel pour l'amour de Marie*	[Mareschal and Chaussard], c. 1504–6	*Faulce trahison, Dieu te mauldie* (theatrical chanson?)[15]
8. *A minuit fut fait un réveil*	[17th c.]	*Quand la bergere va aux champs*
9. *Or nous dites Marie*	[Vve. Trepperel?], c. 1515	*Helas je l'ay perdue*
10. *Joseph est bien marié*	[Vve. Trepperel?], c. 1515	*Jolyet est marié* (theatrical chanson; *branle*)
11. *Une jeune pucelle*	[16th c.]	*Une jeune fillette de noble cœur* (1557)
12. *Voici le jour solemnel*	[16th c.]	*Quand ce beau printemps je voy,* by Pierre de Ronsard (1587)
13. *A la venuë de Noel*	[*Livre de noëls*], Paris, B.N. f. fr. 2368 (c. 1483–98)	None known
14. *Quand Dieu nâquit à Noel,* by François Colletet	Colletet, 1665	*Quand la Mer rouge apparût* (air à boire)
15. *Grace soit renduë,* by Jehan Tisserand	Tisserand, after 1519[16]	None known
16. *Je me suis levé par un matinet*	[16th c.]	*Je me suis levé par un matinet*

10. This noel also appears with the titles *Ah ma voisine* and *O ma voisine*.

11. For the information in this table, we have used Block wherever possible because she lists primary sources to support her statements. Block supplies all the information for Noels 3, 6, 7, 9, 10, and 13 but the type of timbre, which is taken from H. Mayer Brown, *The Early French Secular Theatre*. Dating for Noels 1, 4, 5, 8, and 16 is from Poulaille, *La grande et belle bible* (though we use Gastoué, *Le cantique populaire*, to date Poulaille's source for Noel 4); timbres for these five noels come from Oudot's 1684 *Grande bible* and are confirmed in most other sources, sometimes with minor variants. Dating and timbre for Noel 11 is from Grimes, citing Poulaille's *La fleur des chansons*. The timbres of Noels 2 and 14 come from their 18th-century authors' anthologies; the type of timbre for Noel 14 comes from Canteloube. All information for Noel 15 is from Gastoué, *Le cantique populaire*.

12. Complete citations can be found in the bibliography.

13. Poulaille (*La grande et belle bible*) gives "Édition gothique, 1520" as his source.

14. This may be the theatrical chanson *Turelure*, named after the refrain of *Nous mismes a jouer* (*Avec la tourloura la, la*). Howard Mayer Brown, *Music in the French Secular Theater, 1400–1550* (Cambridge, Mass.: Harvard University Press, 1963), 277, no. 393d.

15. This may be the theatrical chanson beginning *Faulx envieux dieu vous mauldie! Vous m'avés la mort au cul mis.* Cited in Brown, 219, no. 132a. No other words or music survives.

16. Gastoué states that this is a reprinting (*Le cantique populaire*, 235); he believes the first printing to be c. 1489–1503.

Sacred Parody in Noel Texts

Almost all noels are *parodies*, songs in which new words are created to replace the original text. Historians today call the borrowed tune a *timbre*. This melody could be a liturgical air or a secular song. Noels based on liturgical chants or hymns are among the earliest and are usually written in Latin.[17] Those based on theatrical chansons, dance songs, and drinking songs are written in the vernacular (either French or a dialect[18]) and form the large majority of the noel repertory; this is the only type represented in Rippert's collection. François Colletet (1628–80), in the preface to his collection of new noel texts (including Noel 14), explains why he changes profane songs to spiritual songs:

> *. . . je me suis advisé, pour vous faire dévotement passer les Advents qui approchent, de convertir ces chansons de dissolution et de débauche, que l'on oit tous les jours dans la ville de Paris, en cantiques de pieté; afin que ceux qui ont offensé Dieu par le chant melodieux de ces airs souvent impudiques, se servent des mesmes airs pour le loüer, et pour reconnaistre en mesme temps leur crime.*

> . . . I got the idea, so that you may spend future Advent seasons devoutly, of converting these songs of dissolution and of debauchery, which one hears every day in the city of Paris, into pious songs, so that those who have offended God with the melodious tunes of these often indecent airs may use the same airs to praise Him and at the same time recognize their crime.

Many composers borrowed not only the melodies but the strophic forms and rhyme/assonance patterns from their models. They also borrowed individual words or whole lines: the first line of Noel 16 copies its timbre, and those of Noels 10 and 11 are closely related. Colletet's parody noel *Quand Dieu nâquit à Noel* (Noel 14) and its timbre *Quand la Mer rouge apparut,* a 17th-century biblical drinking song,[19] have the same syllable count, first word, and rhyme scheme except in the fragmented lines 7–9. The scansion matches in only a few lines, which is common for noels (for more on scansion, see chap. 4 and app. 4). In the following comparison, letters in parentheses indicate the rhyme scheme (italicized for feminine rhymes) and diagonal slashes show the scansion:

Noel 14: Timbre		Noel 14: Parody	
Quand la Mer rouge / apparut	(a)	Quand Dieu nâquit / à Noel	(a)
A la trou-/ pe noire,	(*b*)	Dedans la Judée,	(*b*)
Pharaon / tout d'abord crut	(a)	On vit ce jour / solennel	(a)
Qu'il fallait / qu'à boire.	(*b*)	La jo-/ ye innondée;	(*b*)
Mais Moï-/ se savait bien	(c)	Il n'étoit petit / ni grand	(c)
Que l'eau / n'était pas du vin,	(c)	Qui n'apportât / son present,	(c)
Il la pa, / pa, pa,	(d)	Et no, no, / no, no,	(d)
Il la sa, / sa, sa,	(d)	Et ne frit, / frit, frit;	(e)
Il la pa, / il la sa,	(d)	Et no, no, / et ne frit,	(e)
Il la passa / toute,	(*e*)	Et n'offrit / sans cesse	(*f*)
Sans en boi-/ r(e) un' goutte.[20]	(*e*)	Toute sa richesse.	(*f*)

---

17. Block, vol. 1, 54.

18. See Block, vol. 1, 36.

19. This very popular timbre was used for a variety of parodies. A drinking song in J.-B.-C. Ballard's *La clef des chansonniers* (1717), 186–7, retains the first line of the biblical timbre: *Quand la Mer rouge apparût Aux yeux de Gregoire, Aussitôt ce buveur crut, Qu'il n'avoit que boire: Mais mon voisin fut plus fin, Voyant que ce n'étoit vin, Il l'a* [sic] *pas, pas, pas, Il l'a sa, sa, sa, Il l'a pas, Il l'a sa, Il l'a passa toute, Sans en boire goute.* These were probably the words associated with the tune in Rippert's day. As late as the French Revolution, Ballard's drinking song was used as the timbre of a parody concerning beheading: *C'est un coup que l'on reçoit / Avant qu'on s'en doute, / A peine on s'en aperçoit / Car on n'y voit goutte. / Un certain ressort caché / Tout à coup étant lâché / Fait tomber, fait sauter, fait voler la tête / C'est bien plus honnête* (reprinted in J. R. H. de Smidt, *Les noëls et la tradition populaire* (Amsterdam: H. J. Paris, 1932), 186).

20. We were unable to locate a 17th-century source for this text. The modern version we quote is from Joseph Canteloube, ed., "Quand Dieu naquit à Noël!" (Paris: Heugel et Cie., 1952), 1.

When the Red Sea / appeared
To the army / black,
Pharaoh / at first believed
That he had / only to drink:
But Moses / knew well
That the water / wasn't wine,
He did pa, / pa, / pa,
He did sa, / sa, sa,
He did pa, / he did sa,
He did pass over it / all,
Without drinking / a drop.

When God was born / on Christmas
In Judea,
One saw on this day / of solemnity
Joy / overwhelming;
There was no one small / or big
Who did not bring / his present,
And did not, / not, / not,
Offer not, / not, not;
And did not, / offer not,
And did not offer / without end
All his riches.

Noels as Popular Poetry

Noels form a small part of the substantial body of *chansons populaires,* musical settings of popular French poetry. Thus noels do not adhere too rigorously to the rules of "proper" poetic writing or text setting. Their lyrics often exhibit faulty prosody, follow rhyme schemes somewhat freely, and show other peculiarities. Refrains, often found in songs of a popular nature, are common in noels. All these traits contribute to the Christmas songs' "rustic" character, deemed so important by J.-J. Rousseau (see his quotation below).

Rhyme Scheme. Chansons populaires often do not follow rhyme schemes strictly, but most songs exhibit a single, overall pattern of rhyme. One of Rippert's noels (Noel 4) is exceptional because it is constructed with two patterns, alternating in groups of stanzas: a *b* a *b* c *d* c d and a a b b *c* d *c* d. The most common pattern used in noels begins (or consists solely of) a b a b, where either a or b is often feminine.

Assonance frequently substitutes for rhyme (only the vowel of the syllable matches, not the following consonants). Noels 5, 6, 7, and 9 provide numerous examples. In the first stanza of Noel 5, the overall pattern is *a* b *a* b c *d* c d (feminine endings italicized). In the seventh stanza, assonance replaces rhyme in lines one and three, and five and seven:

Noel 5: Stanza 1		Noel 5: Stanza 7
Chantons je vous prie	(*a*)	Quant ils furent au temple
Noel hautement,	(b)	Trestous assemblés,
D'une voix jolie,	(*a*)	Etant tous ensemble
En solemnisant,	(b)	En troupe ordonné,
De Marie pucelle	(*c*)	La verge plaisante
La conception,	(d)	De Joseph fleurit,
Sans originelle	(*c*)	Et à même instance
Maculation.	(d)	Porta fleur et fruit.

Assonance plays a large part in the Happy Shepherds Noel 1. All feminine lines retain the vowel *o,* and most include a crisp *t* among the final consonants: *côte, grotte, décrotte, cotte, porte,* etc. The final line (end of the refrain) softens the consonant to a single *r* for the gentle question *Le verrons-nous encore?* (Will we see Him yet?).

The flexible rhyme schemes used in noels are probably best demonstrated by Mary's Narrative Noel 9. Almost all masculine pairs of this noel rhyme or use assonance, while the feminine pairs variably employ rhyme, assonance, or no coordinating device at all. Take for example the following excerpt:

Or nous dites Marie
Les neuf nois accomplis,
Nâquit le fruit de vie
Comme l'Ange avoit dit? (Stanza 13)

Or nous dites Marie
Du lieu imperial,
Fut-ce en chambre parée,
Où en palais royal? (15)

Oüi, sans nulle peine
Et sans oppression,
Nâquit de tout le monde
La vrai Redemption. (14)

En une pauvre étable
Ouverte à l'environ,
Où n'avoit feu ni flamme,
Ni latte, ni chevron. (16)

Textual Repetition. Several forms of repetition are found in the texts of Rippert's noels. The word *bis* following a line (Noels 8 and 10) calls for the text to be repeated immediately, here to new music. "Linked stanzas" are created by the repetition of one or more of a stanza's lines in the following stanza (Noels 1 and 16).

A single syllable is repeated motivically several times in two noels. In Noel 6 the sounds *don* and *la* are repeated; in Noel 14 first one and then another syllable is sung several times.

Textual refrains of one to three lines join the lyrics of five of Rippert's 16 noels. Four of the refrains conclude stanzas (Noels 1, 10, 15, and 16), while one starts the stanza (Noel 9). The refrains of Noels 1, 15, and 16 stand out because at least one line contrasts in syllable count with the non-refrain lines. Depending on the particular noel, refrain lines may or may not relate in rhyme or assonance to any of the lines that come before.

Prosody. A particularly rustic trait of *chansons populaires* is the dropping of a final soft *e* before a consonant. In Oudot's version of the Love of Mary Noel 7, the third line, *Quand elle porta le fruit de vie,* contains an extra syllable. The soft *e* concluding *elle* presumably was not pronounced; this is confirmed by Ballard's *Chants des noëls,* which reads *ell'* instead of *elle.* Another example occurs in the penultimate stanza of Oudot's version of Noel 5, where the soft *e* must be dropped in four lines: *Ell' fut.*

Conversely, soft *e*'s that would normally be elided must sometimes be pronounced to fill out the poetic line correctly. Oudot's *Grandes bibles* give the fourth line of Joseph's Noel 10 as *D'être mere et pucelle;* the concluding *e* of *mere* must be pronounced to retain the seven-syllable lines of the lyrics. Ballard's version contains an extra syllable so that the soft *e* is properly elided: *Que d'être mer(e) et pucelle.*

Simplicity and Rusticity in Noel Subjects

Besides sharing the rustic characteristics of the *chansons populaires,* noels tell stories of simple shepherds and shepherdesses going to visit Mary, Joseph, and the Child. Many are named for the stereotyped personages of French pastoral songs and plays from the 14th through 18th centuries: Guillot, Margot, Marion, Perronnelle, and Robin appear in the texts of Noels 1, 3, and 8. Shepherds in the noels play musical instruments, many of rustic origin: *bussine* (Noel 3); *chalumeau, tabourin, rebec, luth, trompette, clairon* (Noel 6); *musette* (Noel 10); *tambour, flageolet, viole, archelet* (Noel 16). The pastoral character of noels was pronounced enough that Jean-Jacques Rousseau thought it worthy of comment in his *Dictionnaire de musique* (Paris, 1767):

> *Les airs des* Noêls *doivent avoir un caractère champêtre et pastoral convenable à la simplicité des paroles, et à celle des bergers qu'on suppose les avoir chantés en allant rendre hommage à l'Enfant Jésus dans la crèche.*

The airs of *Noels* should have a rustic and pastoral character suited to the simplicity of the words, and to [the simplicity] of the shepherds who are supposed to have sung them while going to pay homage to the Baby Jesus in the manger.

A good example of such a noel is Noel 3, *Laissez paître vos bêtes*. Rustic humor is used in the first 7-line stanza, where a nightingale "preaches and chatters so much" that it gives a shepherd a headache. The next nine stanzas continue with a bucolic romp of shepherds and shepherdesses (the full text from Oudot's 1684 *Grande bible* is translated below). The petition of the final stanza, more serious in tone, seems to be spoken by those singing the noel, rather than by the characters in the story. Most noel texts end with some kind of plea expressed in the first person plural: "Now let us . . . ."

NOEL 3 *Laissez paître vos bêtes*

Let your animals graze,
Shepherds, by mountains and by valleys;
Let your animals graze,
And come to sing "Noel."

I heard the nightingale singing,
Who sang a song so new,
So good, so beautiful, so resonant;
It gave me a headache,
So much it preached and chattered.
Then I took my staff
To go to see Naulet.

I asked the shepherd Naulet:
"Have you heard the nightingale,
So pretty, who twittered
Up there on the thorn-bush?"
"Yes," he said, "I heard it.
I took my trumpet
And rejoiced."

We all sang a song;
The others came at the sound.
Now, get up, let's dance! You take Alison,
I will take Guillemette,
And Margot will take fat Guillot.
Who will take Perronnelle?
That will be Talebot.

Let's talk no more, we dally too much,
Let's go quickly! Run fast!
Come quickly, Margot! "Wait, Guillot,
I have broken my strap;
I must repair my wooden shoe."
"Now, take this cord,
It will serve you well enough."

"Why, Guillot, aren't you coming?"
"Yes, I am going very slowly;
You don't understand at all my situation:
I have at my heels the mules,
Which is why I can no longer go quickly.
The chills took me
In going to escape." [21]

March ahead, poor mule driver,
And lean on your staff;
And you, Coquart, old oaf,
You should have had great shame
To grimace thus,
And should have realized it,
At least in front of the people.

We ran with such stiffness [from the cold]
To see our sweet Redeemer
And Creator and Maker.
He had (God knows it)
Very great need of clothes:
He lay in the manger
On a little bit of hay.

His mother was with him.
An old man who gave them light
Bore no resemblance to the Child:
He was not his father;
I saw the Child was too good and handsome.
He resembled his Mother;
He is yet more beautiful.

---

21. The final two lines of the sixth stanza seem to be nonsense, perhaps garbled in the noel's early history. Another possible translation is "The mules took me by surprise In going to escape" (*prendre quelqu'un à froid* = to catch someone off guard). NTC's New College French and English Dictionary (Lincolnwood, Ill.: National Textbook Company, 1991), 115.

Now, we had a large bundle
Of food to make a banquet,
But the dandy of Jean Huguet
And a large whippet dog
Saw the pot uncovered.
But this was done by the shepherdess
Who left the door open.

Let us not stop rejoicing;
I will give him an ewe;
To the little son a thrush
Perronnelle gave to him;
And Margot gave him some milk,
A bowl full to the top,
Covered with a lid.

Now let us all beg the King of Kings,
Who gives us all a good Christmas
And good peace from our misdeeds,
That he not remember
Our sins, but give pardon
To those in Purgatory,
To erase our sins. And so be it.

Laissez paître vos bêtes, like most of the noels in Rippert's collection, deals with only a small portion of the Christmas story. Its main focus is the simple characters themselves and how they react to the wondrous news of Christ's birth. A more complete account of the Christmas story is provided by the oldest of Rippert's noels, *A la venuë de Noel* (Noel 13). Though more serious in tone, it is still simple and unaffected, and expresses pious reverence for the Holy Family.

NOEL 13 *A la venuë de Noel*

At the coming of Christmas,
Each one should heartily rejoice,
Because it's a new testament
That all the world must heed.

When by his pride Lucifer
Stumbled into the abyss,
We all were going to Hell,
But the Son of God redeemed us.

Within a Virgin He cast his shadow,
And in her body He wished to lie:
The night of Christmas she gave birth
Without suffering pain and anguish.

As soon as God was born,
The angel went to tell it to the shepherds,
Who took to singing
A melody that was graceful.

After a very little time,
Three kings came to adore him,
Bringing him myrrh and incense
And gold, which is very praiseworthy.

To God they came to present it,
And when it came time for their return,
Three days and three nights without cease
Herod had them pursued.

A star guided them,
Which came from the East,
Which to one and all showed
The direct road to Bethlehem.

We must certainly
Take the way and the road,
Because it shows us truly
Where Our Lady must lie.

There they saw the sweet Jesus Christ
And the Virgin who carried Him,
He who made the entire world
And brought the sinners back to life.

It was clear that He loved us
When He was put on the Cross for us:
May God the Father, who created all,
Give us at the end Paradise.

Let us all pray that at the last day,
When all the world must end,
That we do nothing of ourselves
To suffer any of Hell's pain.

Amen. Noel, Noel, Noel.
I cannot restrain myself any longer,
And must sing this noel
When I see my Savior come.

Noel pour l'amour de Marie (Noel 7) portrays Mary and Joseph as common folk who search in vain for lodging when she is about to give birth. The final few stanzas advise people to bear their difficulties patiently and ask for guidance so they may enter Paradise.

NOEL 7 *Noel pour l'amour de Marie*

"Noel" for the love of Mary
We will sing joyously:
When she carried the fruit of life,
This was for our salvation.

Joseph and Mary went away
One night very late to Bethlehem;
Those who kept lodgings
Did not think very highly of them.

They went through the town
And asked for lodging from door to door;
At that time the Virgin Mary
Was nigh ready to have the Child.

They went to the home of a rich man
To ask humbly for lodging,
And they were answered in sum:
"Have you many horses?"

"We have an ox and a donkey,
See them here."
"You seem to be nothing but vagrants;
You will not lodge here."

They went to another man's house
To ask lodging in return for money,
And they were told again:
"You will not stay here."

Joseph then saw a man
Who called him a wretched peasant:
"Where do you want to take this woman,
Who is not more than 15 years old?"

Joseph goes regarding Mary,
Who has a very sorrowful heart,
Saying to her: "My dear love,
We will have nowhere else to stay."

"I saw over there an old stable,
Let us lodge there for now."
At that time the Virgin Mary
Was nigh ready to have the Child.

At midnight this night,
The sweet Virgin had the Child;
Her dress was not fur-lined
To wrap Him warmly.

She put Him in a manger
On only a little hay,
A stone under His head
To rest the almighty King.

Very dear people, do not be upset
If you live very poorly;
If fortune is against you,
Take everything patiently,

In memory of the Virgin,
Who took poor lodgings
In an open stable
That was not closed in front.

Now let us beg the Virgin Mary,
That she be willing to implore her Son,
That He help us live such a life
That we may be able to enter Paradise.

If we could be there once,
Never would we lack anything again.
Thus was lodged our master,
Sweet Jesus, in Bethlehem.

Cries of *Noel! Noel!* in the first stanza of Noel 7 and the last stanza of Noel 13 are common, as are variations of similar formulas. The idea *Chanter noel* (Sing noel) begins Noels 3, 5, 7, and dominates the refrain of Noel 16. The line *Chantons je vous (en) prie* (Let us sing, I beg you) begins Noel 5 and the earlier version of Noel 9.[22]

The Noel and Dance

According to Margit Sahlin, the connection of dancing with Christmastime was already strong before the noels appeared. She says that during the "dancing season" of winter, popular dancing took place especially on Christmas and New Year's Day, and that pious songs for Christmas dancing were composed by the Franciscans in an effort to popularize religion.[23] Douglas Jay Rahn points out that the Latin noels in a French manuscript dating c. 1491–98 make repeated reference to the *tripudium*, the usual step in religious dance.[24] The particular choreographies for church dancing varied from region to region, but in most dances the participants, who sometimes included the clergy themselves, held hands in a ring or formed a line of couples.[25]

Though dancing was part of the ritual in many churches, not all dancing was welcome. According to E. Louis Backman, the clergy objected "to those forms of the dance which were vicious and indecent, with improper songs, and to the participation of women and the dancing together of men and women."[26] One reason for these abuses was the pagan influence of the newly-converted trying to retain the practices of their cults.[27] Noels, being a popular genre, were probably associated with these "indecent" dances.

Many of the 15th- and 16th-century noels are associated with dancing. The *basse dance* is the choreography most often mentioned in conjunction with early noels and their timbres.[28] Many chanson timbres for noels in Pierre Sergent's [1537?] collection are given specific choreographies in [Jaques Moderne's] *S'Ensuyvent plusieurs basses dances* (1530s–40s). Some are shown elsewhere to be *branles, pavanes,* Morris dances, or hay dances.[29] Many are listed among the dances in a manuscript of Rabelais' *Pantagruel* (before 1654), where Rabelais describes entertainment after a banquet in the fictitious country of Lanternois:

> *Le soupper finy, furent les tables levées. Lors, les menestriers plus que devant mélodieusement sonnantz, fut par la Royne commancé ung bransle double, auquel tous . . . ensemble dansèrent. Depuys se retira la Royne en son siège; les aultres aux dives sons des bouzines dansarent diversement, comme vous pourrez dire: . . .*[30]

Supper finished, the tables were taken up [to clear the floor for dancing]. Then, with the minstrels playing more melodiously than before, the Queen began a *branle double*, which all

---

22. Noel 9 is found in two main versions. The earlier form begins *Chantons je vous en prie* and is the one given by most noel publishers, including Sergent, Ballard, and Oudot. The other form begins *Or nous dites*, the opening of the earlier version's eighth quatrain. This version is given by Rippert and used by Pellegrin for his noel parodies.

23. Margit Sahlin, *Étude sur la carole médiévale* (Uppsala: Almquist and Wiksells, 1940), 181.

24. *S'Ensuivent aucuns ditez et chançons faitez en l'onneur de la nativité de Jhésu Crist començans par noel* (Paris, Bibliothèque de l'Arsenal, MS 3653). In Rahn, 48.

25. E. Louis Backman, *Religious Dances in the Christian Church and in Popular Medicine* (Westport, Conn.: Greenwood Press Publishers, 1952; reprint, 1977), 91 (page citations are to reprint edition).

26. Backman, 154.

27. Backman, 154. See also Sahlin, 33.

28. Block's extensive bibliography (vol. 2) for each noel in Sergent's collection made this observation possible.

29. We credit Block's extensive bibliography (vol. 2).

30. François Rabelais, *Le Cinquième et Dernier Livre des faicts et dits héroïques du bon Pantagruel,* chap. 32 bis., in *Œuvres complètes*, ed. Guy Demerson (Paris: Editions du Seuil, 1973), 927. The quoted passage is not in the 1564 (posthumously printed) publication, but appears in a manuscript (not autograph, thought to date before 1564) of the *Cinquième livre* at the Bibliothèque nationale. (In modern editions of the fifth book, chapter 32 bis is often omitted from the main text but included in an appendix or separate section.)

. . . danced together. After the queen retired to her seat, the others, to the divine sounds of the buccines,[31] performed diverse dances, as you might name: . . . [a long list of titles follows, many from Moderne's *basse dance* manual, including *A la venuë de Noel*].

The Noel in the Church

In 1492 Jehan Tisserand, the author of Noel 15, founded the refuge of Ste. Madeleine for *filles repenties* (repentent girls), who were consequently called the *Madelonnettes*. The first extant printed noels, *S'Ensuivent les noëls tresexcelens* (published by Guillaume Guerson in Paris between 1495 and 1502), were sung by these *filles rendues a Paris* (redeemed girls of Paris) in their devotions.[32] Rippert's Noel 13, *A la venuë de Noel,* is the second in this collection. Noels are presented as private devotions in a c. 1500 noel text that mentions ladies singing noels *secreto et sub ocio* (secretly [i.e., privately] and at leisure).[33]

Because of the popularity of noels, the Franciscans brought them into the church to attract attendance, with varying degrees of tolerance from other orders.[34] The 16th-century humanist scholar and priest Erasmus criticized secular influences in the Church, influences that came from genres such as the noel, usually based on secular song:

> *Nunc sonis nequissimus aptanture verba sacra, nihilo magis decore. . . . Interdum nec verba silentur impudica cantorum licentia. Haec si leges negligunt, tamen oportebat advigilare sacerdotes et episcopos. . . .*[35]

Now sacred words are joined to the most worthless music. . . . And occasionally the words [of the sacred texts] are left out through shameless licenses taken by the singers. If laws neglect this [situation], it is up to the priests and bishops to exercise vigilance. . . .

Jan de Tournes, publisher of an early collection of noel texts, objected so strongly to such abuses that he composed his own, presumably dignified, collection of sacred songs (Lyon, 1557). In his preface, he criticized those who chose "lewd and detestable songs" for their noel melodies:

> *Ce que ont fait noz anciens peres, composant plusieurs hymnes et cantiques, tant en latin qu'en françois, contenant le mystere de sa nativité et de ses saints, desquelz la feste est reverée au temps de son advenement. Et se [???] sur le chant de plusieurs hymnes qui se chantent en l'église, ausquels on avoit grande reverence. Depuis sont venus plusieurs rythmiques, qui à leurs plaisirs ont composé plusieurs noelz, sur le chant d'aucunes chansons lubriques et detestables, y ajoutant propos facecieux et loings du saint mystere plus mouvant à derision qu'à devotion.*[36]

What our forefathers did was to compose many hymns and canticles, both in Latin and in French, about the mysteries of His nativity and of His saints whose feasts are revered at the time of His coming. And these [were set?] to the tune of many hymns sung in church, which were greatly revered. Then came a number of versifiers who took pleasure in composing noels

---

31. According to Randle Cotgrave, *A Dictionarie of the French and English Tongues* (London, 1611), a *buccine* is a "cornet, or trumpet for the warres."

32. Rahn, 54.

33. Manuscript Paris, Bibliothèque de l'Arsenal, 3653 (c. 1500). Text and translation in Rahn, 48.

34. Block, vol. 1, 99.

35. Erasmus, *Institutio christiani matrimonii* (1525), preface. In *Opera omnia* (Leyde: J. Clericus), vol. 5, 718c. Jean-Claude Margolin, *Erasme et la musique* (Paris, 1965), gives the original Latin (from *Opera omnia*) and a French translation, 16–17. Block gives the above English translation, vol. 1, 3.

36. Jan de Tournes, *Noelz vieux et nouveaux en l'honneur de la nativité Jesus Christ, et de sa tresdigne mere* (Lyon, 1557). In Block, vol. 1, 112.

to the tune of lewd and detestable songs, adding to them facetious matter far removed from the Holy Mystery, more likely to inspire derision than devotion.

Not everyone associated noels with shameful songs. Estienne Pasquier (1529–1615), a royal councilor and general lawyer, appreciated the Christmas tunes as familiar songs in their own right. When recalling the family evenings of his youth, Pasquier told how noels were sung every evening in homes and were still sung during the offering at high mass on Christmas Day:

> *Et en ma jeunesse c'estoit une coustume que l'on avoit tournée en ceremonie, de chanter tous les soirs presque en chaque famille des noëls, qui estoient chansons spirituelles faites en l'honneur de nostre Seigneur. Lesquelles on chante encore en plusieurs églises pendant que l'on celebre la grand'messe le jour de Nouël, lors que le prestre reçoit les offrandes.*[37]

And in my youth, in almost in every family, it was a custom that had become a ceremony, to sing every evening some noels, which were spiritual songs written in honor of our Lord, which are still sung in many churches while celebrating the high mass of Christmas Day, when the priest receives the offerings.

By the end of the 16th century, noels had gained acceptance in many churches. Organ settings of noels began to appear, and these continued to be written well into the 18th century.[38] Much of the production of parody noels had ceased by 1625,[39] and a smaller corpus of the most revered noels, of which Rippert's collection provides a good example, was used repeatedly for musical arrangements.

In 1685, Nicolas Lebègue (1630–1702) included 14 noel arrangements in his third book of organ pieces.[40] Eleven of these are based on just five noels, found also in Rippert's anthology. Jean-François Dandrieu (1664–1733) included 15 noels present in Rippert's collection;[41] André Raison (a. 1650–1719) included 12;[42] and Louis-Claude Daquin (1694–1772), five.[43] Daquin wrote his arrangements for organ or harpsichord, but said most could be played on violins, flutes, and oboes. The inclusion of the harpsichord as an alternative to the organ in the collections of Lebègue, and Raison shows these arrangements were intended for home as well as church use.

The first composer to set noels for groups of instruments may have been Marc-Antoine Charpentier (1634?–1704). In the late 17th century he arranged three noels (also later arranged by Rippert) for flutes, strings, and organ, and entitled them simply *Noëls sur les instruments.*[44] Around the same time, Charpentier's *Messe de minuit pour Noël*[45] included polyphonic settings of ten noels (nine in Rippert) to be used in the Latin mass.

37. Estienne Pasquier, *Les recherches de la France*, book 4, chap. 16 (Paris: Laurens Sonnius, 1571); reprint, reviewed, corrected, and reordered (Paris: Louys Billaine, 1665), 351 (page citations are to 1665 edition). Block, in her bibliography, also cites another earlier edition, published in Orléans by Pierre Trepperel in 1557. We do not know if this passage occurs in this edition or whether the 1571 volume was a revision or simply a reprinting.

38. Eileen Morris Guenther, "Composers of French Noël Variations in the 17th and 18th Centuries," part 1, *The Diapason* 65, no. 1 (1973): 1.

39. Bruce W. Wardropper, "The Religious Conversion of Profane Poetry," in *Studies in the Continental Background of Renaissance English Literature: Essays presented to John L. Lievsay*, ed. Dale B. J. Randall (Durham, N.C., 1977), 209.

40. Nicolas Lebègue, *Troisieme livre d'orgue . . . et tous les noëls les plus connus . . . que l'on peut jouer sur l'orgue et le clavecin* (Paris, 1685), ed. Norbert Dufourq as *Noëls variés*, Orgue et Liturgie no. 16 (Paris: Éditions musicales de la Schola cantorum et de la Procure générale de musique, 1952).

41. Jean-François Dandrieu, *Noëls . . . mis pour l'orgue et pour le clavecin* [?1721–33], ed. Gaston Litaize and Jean Bonfils as *Noëls*, L'Organiste Liturgique nos. 19–20 (Paris: Editions musicales de la Schola cantorum et de la Procure générale de musique, 1955).

42. André Raison, *Second livre d'orgue* (Paris, [1714]).

43. Louis-Claude Daquin, *Nouveau livre de noëls pour l'orgue et le clavecin* (Paris, c. 1740), ed. Norbert Dufourcq, Félix Raugel, and Jean de Valois as *Nouveau livre de noëls*, Orgue et liturgie nos. 27–8 (Paris: Éditions musicales de la Schola cantorum et de la Procure générale de musique, n.d.).

44. Marc-Antoine Charpentier, *Noëls sur les instruments* (Paris, Bibliothèque nationale, MS Rés., Vm¹ 259, tome 5). These were probably composed in the early 1690's.

45. Marc-Antoine Charpentier, *Messe de minuit pour Noël*, ed. H. Wiley Hitchcock (St. Louis, Mo.: Concordia Publishing House, 1962). The mass was probably composed in the early 1690's.

They were sung by solo voices and mixed chorus and accompanied by flutes, strings, and organ. For the offertory, violins played a simple version of the Grazing Noel 3.

Michel-Richard de Lalande (1657–1726) was another arranger of noels for instruments. In his *Symphonie des noëls*,[46] he used violins, oboes, flutes, and basso continuo to play 13 noels included by Rippert a few years earlier. Perhaps Lalande's "flutes" included recorders and transverse flutes as in the Christophe picture on our title page.

Congregational singing of noels may have occurred during offertory (as in Estienne Pasquier's quote above). Organ arrangements appear to have been played as preludes or postludes to services, and between services.[47] The arrangements in Lalande's *Symphonie des noëls* were played in the Royal Chapel on Christmas Eve, from the end of Matins until the start of the Midnight Mass.[48]

Musical Style in Noel Settings

Lebègue's organ arrangements of 1685 are simple, three-voice settings, but later organists introduced occasional echoes, phrase extensions, florid turns, and long runs. *Doubles* and *Diminutions* ornamented complete stanzas with almost steady eighths or sixteenths, sometimes mixed with quicker values.[49] This bolder musical style elicited complaints from the clergy. In 1725, the year Rippert's collection was published, the Synod of Avignon announced that noels in church,

> . . . *jusqu'ici tolerés, sont prohibés par ce saint synode, parce qu'ils rabaissent les saints mystères, par des mélanges de choses risibles, beaucoups de vains bavardages, et des jeux malsonnants.*[50]

> . . . tolerated up until now, are prohibited by this holy synod, because they debase the holy mysteries, by mixing ridiculous things, many vain chatterings, and ill-sounding organ registrations.

Early 18th-century settings of noels for singing remained simple. To the old monophonic tunes, Ballard in 1704 added basses similar to those in his publishing company's brunette collections of the same period. Some basses were sung while others served as an unfigured accompaniment. Pellegrin in 1718 and 1728 published many of the same melodies with his own sung bass and new lyrics.

The instrumental arrangements of Rippert and Lalande reflect the simplicity of the vocal sources. The second flute parts in Rippert's duets are similar to the sung basses of Ballard and Pellegrin. Rippert's second flute moves chiefly in thirds with the first until the end of each poetic line, where it supplies the necessary harmonic underpinning. In the *Advertissement*, which appears only in the Lyon volume, Rippert describes his difficulties in finding suitable second parts and begs for tolerance of his few small licenses.

46. Michel-Richard de Lalande, *Symphonie des noëls* from *Recueil d'airs detachez et d'airs de violons* (1727), ed. Rudolf Ewerhart as *Symphonie des Noëls für Melodieinstrumente (Blockflöten, Flöten, Oboen, Violinen) und Basso continuo,* 3 vols. (Celle, Germany: Moeck, n.d.).

47. See Jean Saint-Arroman, *L'interpretation de la musique française 1661–1789* (Paris: Librairie Honoré Champion, 1985), 231.

48. Block, vol. 1, 113.

49. These organ pieces are discussed in depth in several articles by organists. See Eileen Morris Guenther, "Composers of French Noël Variations in the 17th and 18th Centuries," parts 1–3, *The Diapason* 65/1 (1973): 1–5; 65/2 (1974): 1–4; 65/3 (1974): 4–5, 13; and Conrad Grimes, "The Noels of Louis-Claude Daquin," *The Diapason* 60/1 (1968): 24–7.

50. Block, vol. 1, 112, citing Amédée Gastoué, *Noël: Origines et développements de la fête* (Paris: Librairie Blond, 1900), 53. Block misinterprets the word *jeux* to mean "games," suggesting the organist used tunes from current stage entertainment instead of the venerated noels from the 16th century. However, *jeux* is also the French word for "organ stops."

2

Noel Forms for Singing, Dancing, and Playing: Renaissance to Baroque

By 1725, many of the noels in Jean-Jacques Rippert's collection had been sung and played for two hundred years. Over this period, changes occurred in the noels' rhythms, bar lines, time signs, phrase lengths, and repeated strains. The 16th century's uniform dance rhythms ordered the free-flowing rhythms of popular song, while the 17th century's classical aesthetics standardized bar lines and forms. In the 18th century, instrumental composers added their individual touches, including whole variations.

Only a handful of Renaissance and Baroque collections give both music and text for noels. One early source includes a melody for Noel 9's timbre, and another gives the melodies for Noels 3, 7, and 13:

(1) Paris, Bibliothèque nationale, fonds fr. 12744-anc. suppl. fr. no. 169 (manuscript, c. 1500). Contains music and text for the chanson *Helas je l'ay perdue*, the timbre for Noel 9.

(2) *La fleur des noelz* (publ. [Jaques Moderne], Lyon, [1535]).[1] Contains music and texts for ten noels. Facsimile pages of the three that appear in Rippert (Noels 3, 7, and 13) are given in appendix 1.

Two 18th-century sources give music and text for all but Rippert's Noels 2 and 14:

(1) *Chants des noëls, anciens et nouveaux de la grande bible, notez avec la basse-continue* (publ. Christophe Ballard, Paris, 1704; reprint 1712). Contains melodies, sung or unfigured continuo basses, and the first few stanzas of 18 noels. For the remaining stanzas, Ballard refers readers to Nicolas Oudot's *Grandes bibles*, which offer only noel texts (the 1684 printing of the *Grande bible* is the chief source of lyrics for our edition in Part II), and to "M.ʳ Pellegrin" (see next source). A facsimile of Ballard's first page (1712 printing) is given in appendix 2.

(2) Simon-Joseph Pellegrin, *Chants des noëls anciens* (Paris, 1718).[2] Contains essentially the same melodies as Ballard (above), but different sung basses and the author's new noel texts. Because the texts are not the traditional ones, this source gives only general help in coordinating old texts and music.

For comparison in this chapter we use these four sources, Rippert's flute duet anthology (facsimiles in app. 3), and the musical arrangements cited in chapter 1.

To help readers compare the musical examples of this chapter, we have transcribed Renaissance sources using modern notation and note values (usually halving those of the original). For all excerpts we use the treble clef and modern key signatures (original minor signatures included only the flatted third, i.e., b-flat for g minor, no flats for d minor). Original clefs, time signs, and starting notes are indicated before the brace in each example.

---

1. The only known surviving copy was purchased by the natural son of Christopher Columbus in 1535 and is held at Seville, Biblioteca Colombina (15.2.16).

2. Ernest Myrand, *Noels anciens de la nouvelle-France* (2nd ed. Quebec: Typ. Laflamme & Proulx, 1907), 123-4, shows the same music to be in the *Noëls nouveaux* section of Pellegrin's *Poésies chrétiennes*, Paris, 1701; reprint, 1706).

Some musical examples in this chapter come from music having no lyrics (such as Nicolas Lebègue's organ solos and Rippert's flute duets). Unless we state otherwise, we underlay these with text [in brackets] from the 1684 edition of Nicolas Oudot's *La Grande bible des noëls*.[3]

NOTE: In our musical examples we line up similar pitches in the different sources so that variants can be seen readily. This means that the sources may not always correspond rhythmically. In example 2.2, for instance, the pitch A (m. 2) is lined up in the three sources, even though this causes a half note (ex. 2.2a) to correspond to a dotted half note (ex. 2.2c); the half note would of course be shorter.

Noel Lines Set to Four Beats of Music

During the 16th century two different forms of a song evidently existed side by side. The one for singing reflected a somewhat improvisatory vocal tradition. Phrases flowed like expressive recitation, stretching out poignant syllables with ornamental pitches, or final rhymes with lengthened values. The form for dancing required more regularity for dancers to time their steps. Each step-unit was danced to a line of poetry, with one note normally set to each syllable and an average of two syllables set to each half- or dotted half-note beat of music. The most common step-units were timed to four beats of music, which would take two measures of Rippert's noels with the 2 and 3/2 signs, and four measures with the 3 sign. Thus most lines were fitted to four beats of music for dancing.

All noels in the two early musical sources use the slashed C sign. Eleven of Rippert's noels remain in their original duple meter but with the 2 sign of late Baroque gavottes, bourrées, and rigaudons. Four take the 3 sign common to late Baroque menuets and Spanish dances. One has the 3/2 sign of late Baroque courantes. The late Baroque meter signs and frequent mid-measure starts make Rippert's pieces resemble the elegant dances by Lully and his followers, but a closer study reveals rustic lyrics set to archaic dance steps. We use the four early noels and a 17th-century one (Noel 14) to demonstrate the structural changes in noels that occurred from the early Renaissance to the late Baroque.

The Coming of Christmas Noel 13 (Duple Meter)

The melody that Moderne published for *A la venuë de Noel* (Noel 13) is not strictly danceable, but the choreography he printed for this same noel in a *basse dance* collection (unfortunately without music) shows it was danced.[4] In the music for Moderne's sung version, the second rhyme of each line pair is lengthened as in a poetic recitation (ex. 2.1a). In an early 17th-century German version with Latin text, only the last rhyme of the stanza is extended (ex. 2.1b). No extra length remains in most late Baroque versions (ex. 2.1c and d).

Bar lines vary among the sources. Moderne uses none. The German (Latin; ex. 2.1b) version sets off poetic lines with bar lines that fit four-beat step-units. Most later French sources, including Ballard, Pellegrin, and Rippert, place bar lines in the middle of lines (see chap. 4), as in gavottes of the late Baroque. These bar lines divide the old dance rhythms, as do those in Rippert's Noels 10, 12, 14, and 16.

---

3. Our editorial procedures for lyrics are explained in the introduction to Part II.

4. [Jaques Moderne], *S'Ensuyvent plusieurs basses dances* (n.p., n.d.), f. B2'; in Block, vol. 2, 16. This was probably published between the late 1530s and early 1540s, Moderne's main period of production.

EXAMPLE 2.1. Four versions of Noel 13.   a. Moderne [1535].   b. *Das Andernacher Gesangbuch* (1608). c. Ballard (1704/12). d. Rippert (1725).

The Love of Mary Noel 7 (Triple Meter)

Moderne's version of *Noel pour l'amour de Marie* (Noel 7; ex. 2.2a) preserves the flowing phrases of the vocal tradition. Expression is heightened in the first eight-syllable line by the long first syllable of *l'amour* and the ornamentation and lengthening of *Marie*, which lasts as long as the previous six syllables. Moderne's rhythms, intended for singing, fit neither duple nor triple meter convincingly. Most later composers set the eight syllables to four measures with the 3 sign (exx. 2.2b andc), making the lines danceable.

EXAMPLE 2.2. Three versions of Noel 7, line 1. a. Moderne [1535]. b. Lebègue (1685). c. Rippert (1725).

The Grazing Noel 3: Strain 1

Laissez paître vos bêtes is the latest of the four early noels; it is called *Noel nouveau* (New noel) by both Moderne and Olivier Arnoullet,[5] and it has features not found in the other three. All lines in the first quatrain are set to four beats of music (ex. 2.3), so that no modification is necessary to accommodate the four-beat step-units. The final quatrain is like the first. (The central three lines of the song are discussed shortly.)

EXAMPLE 2.3. Four versions of Noel 3, strain 1, lines 1–2. a. Moderne [1535]. b. Lebègue (1685). c. Ballard (1704/12). d. Rippert (1725).

---

5. Olivier Arnoullet, publ., *Noelz nouveaulx nouvellement faitz et composez* (Lyon, [1517-67]). In Block, vol. 2, 102.

Among the versions of Noel 3's first quatrain in example 2.3, only the rhythms within beats vary. The rests, bar line positions, and meter signs show several ways that bar lines were fitted to early songs that start before the beat. The frequent conflicts that result between musical and textual accents are discussed in chapter 4.

Mary's Narrative Noel 9

Baroque composers used various rhythms for *Or nous dites Marie* (Noel 9; ex. 2.4). In the late 17th century, Marc-Antoine Charpentier set his first line to four beats of music in duple meter, and Nicolas Lebègue used four beats in triple meter. But Ballard, Rippert, and most 18th-century arrangers set the lines to six beats in triple time, as for the 15th-century *basse dance*. (Ballard's different lyrics are discussed shortly.) In the 15th-century *basse dance*, four dance motions were made to every six musical beats. With Rippert's music in 3/2 time (three half-note beats to the measure), dancers would move as in 6/4 time (two dotted–half-note motions in the measure; see chap. 3 for dance descriptions).

EXAMPLE 2.4. Noel 9, line 1. a. Charpentier, *Messe de minuit pour Noël* (early 1690s?). b. Lebègue (1685). c. Ballard (1704/12). d. Rippert (1725), transcribed into black notation.

The form of Noel 9 that we found in all 18th-century sources begins with the second musical strain of the timbre chanson and continues with the first. Except for a florid ornament that expresses the poet's suffering, the chanson's first strain (ex. 2.5a) has almost the same rhythm as Rippert's second strain (ex. 2.5b). Except for the genders of the line endings and a two-note ornament, the chanson's second strain (ex. 2.6a) has essentially the rhythm of the noel's first strain (ex. 2.6b). The chanson's first strain and the noel's second strain begin gently, consist of four lines of music, and end decisively. The chanson's second strain and the noel's first strain begin with an upward leap, consist of two lines of music repeated with new text, and end less decisively. The chanson's odd number of quatrains allow it to end decisively with the music of its first strain.

EXAMPLE 2.5. *Helas* chanson, strain 1; Noel 9, strain 2.[6] a. Paris, Bibliothèque nationale, MS fonds fr. 12744-anc. suppl. fr. no. 169, lines 1-2; our transposition. b. Rippert (1725), mm. 9-12.

EXAMPLE 2.6. *Helas* chanson, strain 2; Noel 9, strain 1. a. Paris, Bibliothèque nationale, MS fonds fr. 12744-anc. suppl. fr. no. 169, lines 5-8; our transposition. b. Rippert (1725), mm. 1-8.

Longer and Shorter Lines in Noels

Though most poetic lines are set to four beats of music, lines having more than four beats can also be danced. The eight-beat lines in Noels 11 and 16 fit two four-beat step-units. The first step would be taken on the first downbeat of Noel 11 and on the first note (mid-measure) of Noel 16. The paired four- and two-beat lines in Noel 12 could be danced to a four- plus a two-beat step-unit. The six-beat lines in Noel 9 could be danced to the four beats of the 15th-century *basse dance* (see below).

Some lines differ in length among the sources. The three lines that make up the central section of Noel 3 differ in Moderne and Ballard (discussed below). The second line of Noel 16 has six beats in Rippert, Ballard, and Pellegrin, but eight in Daquin, Dandrieu, and Lalande. A shortened line in Noel 6 causes later lines to start at mid-

---

6. This chanson is also transcribed in Block, vol. 2, 71–2, and Conrad Grimes, "The Noels of Louis-Claude Daquin," *The Diapason* 60, no. 1 (1968): 25.

measure in Rippert but not in Ballard and Pellegrin. A similar shortening in Noel 15 makes the refrain start at mid-measure; if the refrain were sung in chorus but not danced, the stanzas would fit the four-beat step-units.

The Grazing Noel 3: Central Three Lines

The central section of *Laissez paître vos bêtes* has three lines set to musical phrases of more than four beats. A suddenly longer musical phrase begun on the downbeat causes the other two phrases in later versions to start after the downbeat. Moderne sets these central lines to six, five, and five beats; Ballard and Rippert set them to seven, four, and five beats (ex. 2.7). Perhaps the three irregular phrases were danced to step-units of mixed lengths. However, they total 16 beats of music and so could be sung across four four-beat step-units, marking different syllables in Moderne and Ballard (ex. 2.8).

EXAMPLE 2.7. Noel 3, central section, line 1. a. Moderne [1535]. b. Ballard (1704/12). c. Rippert (1725).

EXAMPLE 2.8. The three central lines of Noel 3 sung across four four-beat step-units (underlines show the dance motions and the musical beats; capital letters show the starts of the poetic lines).

	Moderne	Ballard
step-unit 1	J'ou-y chan-ter le	J'ay oüy chan-ter __
step-unit 2	ros-si-gnol Qui chan-toit	le ros-si-gnol, Qui chan-toit
step-unit 3	ung chant si nou-veau Si hault si	un chant si nou-veau, Si haut, si
step-unit 4	beau si re-so-nau __ (Il)	beau, si ré-son-neau __; (Il)

Birth of God Noel 14: Strain 2

Around 1600 the melody of *Quand Dieu nâquit à Noel* (Noel 14) appears in a keyboard *allemande* having four-beat lines through both strains.[7] In the second strain of later versions, several very short lines of repeated textual fragments break the four-beat pattern

---

7. Willam Browne, *Allemando di Guillermo Bruno alias Janetton*, in *Spanish Netherlands Keyboard Music*, ed. Richard Veudome and Colin Good, vol. 2 (Oxford: John Brennan, 1993), 26–7.

(ex. 2.9). These fragments could be danced to one- or two-beat step-units, though we have found no evidence that noels were danced in the 17th century.

EXAMPLE 2.9. Noel 14, strain 2. a. William Browne, *Allemande* [1620?]. b. Rippert (1725), with lyrics from (1) Colletet's noel parody (1665);[8] (2) its biblical timbre (1665);[9] and (3) a secular drinking song in J.-B.-C. Ballard's *La clef des chansonniers* (1717), 186–7. c. Daquin (c. 1740).

---

8. In François Colletet, *Noels nouveaux et cantiques spirituels* (Paris, 1665), 16–19.

9. In Joseph Canteloube, ed., "Quand Dieu naquit à Noël!" (Paris: Heugel et Cie., 1952), 1.

Even though noels may not have been danced in the 17th century, most lines in Rippert's five noels of that period fit the four-beat dance structure. These include Noels 1 and 8 (all lines) and Noel 14 (all but the fragmented lines). Throughout Noels 2 and 4, a line of four beats is paired with a line of two beats.

Noel Stanzas and Strains

In the late 17th century the classical ideals of uniformity, variety, regularity, order, and proportion shaped the rooms and gardens at Louis XIV's summer palace at Versailles. They also shaped the court poetry, dance, and the music of the court dance songs.[10] The binary form in music was admired for the symmetry of its repeated strains, which suited the *belle danse* (beautiful dance) choreographies of the early 18th century. In these dances, both strains were normally repeated and then the whole piece was played again, with both strains repeated.

In instrumental arrangements, repeated strains lengthen the performance time of the music, which would otherwise be played only once unless the stanzas were repeated with variations. The repeat signs differ among 18th-century musical settings, so modern players may omit them in Rippert's noels where the popular lyrics show no new text. Dividing the four lines of the 15th-century Noel 7 into two strains and repeating both with their original texts, as Rippert does, is musically and poetically tedious, and sacrifices the rhyme scheme, the old dance rhythm, and the flow of the story:

Noel pour l'amour de Marie	"Noel" for the love of Mary
Nous chanterons joyeusement,	We will sing joyously;
Noel pour l'amour de Marie	"Noel" for the love of Mary
Nous chanterons joyeusement,	We will sing joyously;
Quand elle porta le fruit de vie	When she carried the fruit of life,
Ce fut pour nôtre sauvement.	This was for our salvation.
Quand elle porta le fruit de vie	When she carried the fruit of life,
Ce fut pour nôtre sauvement.	This was for our salvation.

Because symmetry was an aesthetic goal of the 17th century, the strains of 17th-century noels may better tolerate repetition.

The Love of Mary Noel 7 and the Coming of Christmas Noel 13 consist of only four lines set to music. Each line has the standard four beats. Each stanza fits the 16-beat sequence of step-units in two of the most popular Renaissance dances described in chapter 3. The duple-meter *pavane* is danced with a pair of (2-beat) step-units and a single (4-beat) step-unit, performed first forward and then backward. The most common triple-meter *basse dance* is danced in multiples of 16 beats.

Several 16th-century noels have two four-line strains of equal length. The first strain has music for only two lines, and this is repeated for two more lines. The four lines of the second strain are not repeated. This structure occurs in Noels 5, 9, 10, and 11. Repeating the second strains of these songs without new text makes them twice as long as the first. Noels 6 and 15 have the same structure except that their second strains cover five and seven lines respectively.

---

10. See Mather and Karns, 8.

Mary's Narrative Noel 9: Three Forms

Noel 9 has three forms. Sergent's version [1537?] includes 43 quatrains set to the music of the 15th-century chanson *Helas je l'ay perdue*. Pellegrin's early 18th-century version begins with the music of the chanson's second strain and the lyrics of Sergent's eighth quatrain. Ballard's version begins with the music of the chanson's second strain but the lyrics of Sergent's first quatrain. First we will review the form of the timbre chanson.

The music of the *Helas* first strain begins gently with a stepwise ascent, ends conclusively, and covers four lines of poetry. The music of its second strain begins dramatically with an upward leap, ends inconclusively, covers two lines of poetry, and is repeated with two further lines. The form is ABA . . . BA, since the full close of A must conclude the song. The poetry is laid out in a quatrain and four octaves, showing that the complete musical form is A / BA / BA / BA / BA. The music for the quatrain begins gently, for the octaves dramatically, and all stanzas end decisively.

Sergent's noel is much longer than the timbre chanson. Its 43 stanzas[11] contain an introduction of three quatrains, a main body of 19 pairs of question and answer quatrains, and a conclusion of two quatrains. Sergent cites the *Helas* chanson as the music for the noel, so the form becomes ABA / 19 x BA / BA. This means that the noel's introduction, *Chantons je vous en prie* (Let us sing I beg you), begins gently and ends fully. Each question, *Or nous dites Marie*, begins dramatically, and each answer ends fully. The conclusion also begins dramatically and ends completely. Oudot's *Grandes bibles* of 1684 and 1727 retain the *Helas* music and Sergent's text. Oudot's initial three quatrains and his first three pairs of question-answer quatrains are given below. The third question-answer pair begins the version we use in our edition.

Chantons je vous en prie,	Or nous dites Marie	Or nous dites Marie
Par exaltation,	Qui fut le messager,	Où étiez-vous alors,
En l'honneur de Marie,	Qui porta la nouvelle,	Quand Gabriël l'Archange
Pleine de grand renom.	Pour le monde sauver?	Vous fit un tel record?
Pour tout l'humain lignage,	Ce fut Gabriël l'Ange,	J'étois en Galilée
Jetter hors de peril,	Qui sans dilation,	Plaisante region,
Fut transmis un message,	Dieu envoya sur terre,	En ma chambre enfermée
A la Vierge de prix.	Par grande compassion.	En contmplation.
Nommée fut Marie	Or nous dites Marie	
Par destination,	Que vous dit Gabriël,	
De royalle lignée:	Quand vous porta nouvelle	
Par generation.	Du vrai Dieu eternel?	
	Dieu soit en toi Marie,	
	Dit sans dilation,	
	Tu és de grace remplie,	
	Et benediction.	

The paired questions and answers were of course the focus of this noel. By the 18th century, most instrumental settings were titled *Or nous dites Marie* and began with the dramatic and inconclusive music of the *Helas* second strain. Presumably the introductory quatrains were dropped.

Simon-Joseph Pellegrin gives this version of the noel music (essentially the same as Ballard's in ex. 2.4c) for his own parody noel, *Ecoutez bien l'histoire d'un Dieu dans le berceau* (Listen well to the story of a God in the cradle). In his many collections with and

---

11. Reprinted in Block, vol. 2, 66–70.

without music (several listed in our bibliography) Pellegrin cites *Or nous dites Marie Où étiez-vous alors* as his timbre.[12] This shows that the shortened version starts with Sergent's and Oudot's eighth and ninth stanzas, perhaps the most appealing of the song:

<table>
<tr><td>Now tell us Mary,</td><td>I was in Galilee,</td></tr>
<tr><td>Where were you then,</td><td>Pleasant region,</td></tr>
<tr><td>When the Archangel Garbriel</td><td>Enclosed in my chamber,</td></tr>
<tr><td>Made you such a visit?</td><td>In meditation.</td></tr>
</table>

Ballard's *Chants des noëls* (1704/12) uses the same music as Pellegrin but the old words, which conflict with the affect of the music. He sets the dramatic opening strain to the once gentle *Chantons je vous en prie* (see ex. 2.4c). This makes Mary's gentle answers leap upward and the urgent questions conclusive.

The Grazing Noel 3: Three Musical Sections

The Grazing Noel 3 has three 16-beat sections that resemble the A / B A start of the early Noel 9 and its timbre. The music of the first section (Rippert's first strain) is repeated with new text for the third section. The contrasting music of the central section begins Rippert's second strain:

> Laissez paître vos bêtes,
> Pastoureaux, par monts et par vaux   } 16 beats/music A
> Laissez paître vos bêtes
> Et venez chanter Nau.

> J'ay oüi chanter le rossignol
> Qui chantoit un chant si nouveau,   } 16 beats/music B
> Si haut, si beau, si résonneau

> Il m'y rompoit la tête
> Tant il préchoit et caquetoit,   } 16 beats/music A
> Adonc pris ma houlette
> Pour aller voir Naulet.

The layout of Noel 3's poetry in early and late sources suggests the first quatrain is played only once, followed by a series of seven-line stanzas: A / BA / BA / BA, etc. Rippert's binary music calls for both the quatrain and the seven-line stanza to be repeated: AA / BA BA.

The Coming of Christmas Noel 13: Double

While the multiple stanzas of noel lyrics told long stories and lent themselves to large forms for dancing, the instrumental settings contained fewer repeats of the stanzas. To lengthen their noel arrangements, organists usually included several variations. The first variation often "doubled" the number of notes with running eighths, as in Lully's first variation of *Les folies d'Espagne* for wind band[13] and Rippert's *Doubles* for Noels 1, 10, 13, and 14. Rippert's *Double* for Noel 13 is typical and closely resembles those of the 18th-century organists Dandrieu and Daquin (ex. 2.10).

---

12. Pellegrin cites the single line *Or nous dites Marie* as the timbre of several other noel parodies, most of which we found in only one of his collections. When the timbre starts with *Or nous dites Marie*, the music and text match as in the early form of the noel.

13. In Mather and Karns, 241.

In contrast, Rippert's flute *Doubles* for the popular brunettes *Le beau berger Tircis* and *L'autre jour ma Cloris* feature florid vocal ornaments that intensify the expression of the syllables (ex. 2.11).[14] Perhaps Rippert and the organists considered running eighths suitably pure and ethereal but florid ornaments too full of amorous longing.

EXAMPLE 2.10. Noel 13 *Double*, mm. 1–4. a. Dandrieu (c. 1721–33). b. Rippert (1725). c. Daquin (c. 1740).

EXAMPLE 2.11. Rippert's ornamentation (1725) for the last two lines of *Le beau berger Tircis*. a. first stanza. b. second *Double*.

---

14. Similar flute *Doubles* for these brunettes are found in Jacques Hotteterre, *Airs et brunettes a deux et trois dessus pour les flutes traversieres* (Paris, n.d.), 11, 70–1, and 79; and Michel Pignolet de Montéclair, *Brunettes anciènes et modernes* (Paris, n.d.), 2–3 (*Le beau berger Tircis* only). For further examples of flute *Doubles* see Betty Bang Mather and David Lasocki, *Free Ornamentation in Woodwind Music: 1700–1775* (New York: McGinnis & Marx, 1976).

3

Dance Steps for Early Noel Melodies

The shepherds and shepherdesses in the 16th-century Grazing Noel 3 and Burghers' Noel 6 celebrate with dancing. As mentioned in chapter 1, the Coming of Christmas Noel 13 appears in a 16th-century manual of *basse dance* choreographies and among the dances performed after a banquet in Rabelais' *Pantagruel*. Many noel timbres were also danced in the early 16th century. The timbre of Joseph's Noel 10 was called a *branle* in 1539.[1] Various timbres in Pierre Sergent's [1537?] noel collection were identified as a *basse dance, pavane, branle, trihory*, Morris dance, or hay dance in other sources.[2] In the 17th and 18th centuries, noels were probably no longer danced.

All of Rippert's 16th-century noels, some with minor alterations, readily fit the structures of dances in the manuals of Thoinot Arbeau,[3] Jaques Moderne,[4] Antonius de Arena,[5] and others. Most of the choreographies in Arbeau's manual are informal ring dances performed by the revelers holding hands in a circle and taking steps chiefly to the side, first left, then right. A few are more formal processionals, performed by rather sedate couples following one another in a line, stepping forward and sometimes backward.

The most common step-unit of the Renaissance dances is the four-beat *double*. In Rippert's music with the 2 sign, a *double* starts on the downbeat or at mid-measure and covers two measures. In his music with the 3 sign, a *double* starts on the downbeat and covers four measures. In his single noel with the 3/2 sign, a *double* starts on the downbeat and covers two measures. Each *double* includes three steps and a *pied joint,* in which one foot is brought to join the other. For a *double* to the left (vice versa for one to the right), the steps are as follows (parenthetical abbreviations for later use):

Count 1. Take a step to the left with the left foot, placing the weight on this foot (L).

Count 2. Take a step to the left with the right foot, placing the weight on this foot (R).

Count 3. Take another step to the left with the left foot, placing the weight on this foot (L).

Count 4. Bring the heel of the right foot to join the heel of the left foot (j), but place no weight on the right foot.

In this chapter we discuss briefly the dances particularly suited to the noels' structures: several duple-meter *branles* (ring dances); the duple-meter *allemande* and *pavane* (processional dances); the *basse dance* (triple-meter processional dance); and the *branle gay* and *galliard* (triple-meter dances with fast kicks). We use Arbeau's treatise as our chief source since it is the most complete, clear, and accessible of the 16th-century dance manuals. We present the dances in their approximate order of difficulty.

---

1. Barthélémy Aneau, in his Christmas play *Chant natal, contenant sept noelz* (Lyon, 1539), identifies the timbre as a *branle*. In Howard Mayer Brown, *Music in the French Secular Theater, 1400-1550* (Cambridge: Harvard University Press, 1963), 244, no. 231c.

2. See Block, vol. 2, under the individual noels.

3. Thoinot Arbeau (pseud. of Jean Tabourot), *Orchesographie* (Lengres: Jehan des Preyz, 1588, 1589, and 1596). In our citations, we refer readers first to the facsimile reprint of the third edition, with preface by François Lesure (Geneva: Minkoff, 1972), and then to a widely available translation of the second edition, that of Mary Stewart Evans, reprinted with additions, new introduction, and notes by Julia Sutton, and Labanotation by Mireille Backer and Julia Sutton (New York: Dover, 1967). Complete titles and information on all three editions can be found in our bibliography.

4. [Jaques Moderne], publ., *S'Ensuyvent plusieurs basses dances tant communes que incommunes* (n.p., n.d.). Summary of informative introduction can be found in Heartz, "The Basse Dance: Its Evolution," 299–303, and all choreographies are given in François Lesure, "Danses et chansons à danser au début du XVIe siècle," in *Recueil de travaux offert à M. Clovis Brunel* (Paris, 1955), 177–83.

5. Antonius de (Antoine) Arena, *Ad suos compagnons*, 1519 or later. In *New Grove Dictionary*, s.v. "Arena, Antonius de," vol. 1, 560.

The Duple-Meter *Branles*

The term *branle* embraces all the ring dances. Arena (1519) discusses three types: the *branle double* (having a single step-unit), the *branle simple* (having two step-units), and the *branle coupé* (having further variety in step-units).[6] Seventy years later (1588) Arbeau describes a total of 24 *branles*. Of these, he says the *branle double, simple, gay,* and *de Bourgogne* normally began dancing festivities (as in Rabelais' *Pantagruel,* where the Queen led the *branle double*). In Arbeau's day the duple-meter *branle double* and *branle simple* (the oldest *branles* at that time) were danced sedately by elderly folk, the triple-meter *branle gay* by young married couples, and the lively duple-meter *branle de Bourgogne* by unmarried swains and lasses.[7]

The Branle double

The *branle double* danced by Rabelais' Queen of Lanternois is the simplest and most basic of the ring dances. Arbeau advises that the more solemnly and ponderously (*gravement et pesamment*) it is performed the better.[8]

The structure of the *branle double* is the simplest and most regular possible. From start to finish, a *double* to the left is followed by one to the right: LRLj—RLRj. Each pair of *doubles* takes four measures of Rippert's noels with the 2 sign. The steps of the right *double* are a little smaller than those of the left, bringing the dancers only partially back to where they started so that the circle rotates slowly clockwise. All Rippert's noels having the 2 sign and four- or eight-bar units fit the structure of the *branle double.*

The Branle simple

The *branle simple,* or "single" *branle,* suits the three-measure units (six-beat lines and line pairs) that make up the 16th-century Solemn Day Noel 12. In this dance a four-beat *double* to the left is followed by a two-beat *simple* (single) to the right:

Count 1. Take a step to the right with the right foot, placing the weight on this foot (R).
Count 2. Bring the heel of the left foot to join the heel of the right foot but place no weight on the left foot (j).

Each *simple* takes one measure of Rippert's noels with the 2 sign. A *double* and *simple* together take three measures. In Noel 12 the two-measure first line, *Voici le jour solemnel,* would be danced to a *double*; the one-measure second line, *De Noel,* to a *simple.* Each six-measure unit would be danced to a *double–simple | double–simple* pattern: LRLj—Rj | LRLj—Rj (vertical strokes show Arbeau's bar lines).

The Branle de Bourgogne

The *branle de Bourgogne* is a lively version of the *branle double* and fits all songs that can be danced as *branles doubles.* Its step-unit is identical to the *double* except on the fourth count, where a *grève* lifts the free foot as in a kick.[9] Arbeau gives a single illustration (fig. 1) for the *grève droite* and *pied en l'air droit*; for both, the right foot is

---

6. Daniel Heartz,"Branle," *New Grove Dictionary,* vol. 3, 203.
7. Arbeau (1596), 69r; Evans/Sutton trans., 129.
8. *Ibid.,* 70v; trans., 131.
9. *Ibid.,* 72v; trans., 134–5.

raised. For the *grève gauche* or *pied en l'air gauch*, the left foot is raised. The foot is raised a little higher for the *grève* than for the *pied en l'air*.

FIGURE 1. Arbeau's illustration of the right (a) and left (b) *grève* or *pied en l'air*. [10]

Mixed Branles

Arena (1519) considers all *branles* having further mixed step-units to be *branles coupés*. Arbeau separates these into a variety of *branles* that mix *pieds en l'air* with *doubles* and *simples* as the music and lyrics require. Each *pied en l'air* takes one beat (half a measure of Rippert's noel music with the 2 sign). With an odd number of *pieds en l'air*, the next step-unit starts at mid-measure. Three examples show the diversity possible:

> <u>Branle de Cassandra</u>: four *doubles, simple, double*.
> <u>Branle de Pinagay</u>: *double, pied en l'air, double*, three *pieds en l'air*, two *doubles*.
> <u>Branle de Charlotte</u>: *double*, two *pieds en l'air*, two *doubles*, two *pieds en l'air, simple*, three
> *pieds en l'air, simple*, three *pieds en l'air, double*.

With such mixes, all songs with the 2 sign could be danced as *branles*. Rippert's lines of eight, six, four, and four beats in the New Morning Noel 16 might be danced:

> *double* L, *double* R, *pieds en l'air* L-R-L R-L-R, *double* L, *double* R

The Duple-Meter Processionals

Some noels fit the structures of more formal processional dances. The *pavane* and *allemande* are Arbeau's duple-meter examples. Both were already old in his day.

The *Pavane*

In the early 16th century, Pierre Attaignant arranged the melody of one early noel (not in Rippert's collection) as a *Pavane à 4*.[11] The only other evidence we have that noels might have been danced as *pavanes* is that the structure of so many fits this dance so well (see Ch. 2). Songs suitable for Arbeau's *pavane* are composed of 16-beat units. This structure is in fact found in all Rippert's noels that fit the simpler *branle double*.

---

10. *Ibid.*, 45v; trans., 87.
11. Vve. Attaignant, *IM 1557-3*. Edited in Marx, *Tabulaturen*, Teil 1, 70, fol. 2' (textless). In Block, vol. 2, 179.

The step-units of Arbeau's *pavane* form a large, balanced structure. Four measures are danced forward, the first step taken with the left foot; then four measures are danced backward with smaller steps, the first step taken with the right foot. Dancers walk with decorum and measured gravity (*honnestement avec une gravité posee*).[12]

A four-measure pattern of two *simples* (ss) and a *double* (d) is repeated through the dance, first forward, then backward. For the first *simple* and first measure of music, the left foot steps forward on the first count and the right joins it on the second. For the second *simple* and second measure, the right foot steps forward and the left joins it. For the first *double* and third and fourth musical measures, forward steps are taken with the left, right, and again left foot, and the right is brought to join the left. When the pattern is repeated in the backward direction, the steps are reversed left and right, and are smaller.

> Measures 1–4. Left ss d forward
> Measures 5–8. Right ss d backward (with reversed and smaller steps)

The first half of the Coming of Christmas Noel 13 fits the forward movements of the *pavane* (ex. 3.1). The second half fits the backward movements. The hierarchy of pairs satisfies because it is so balanced. For Moderne's eight stanzas for this song, the *pavane* choreography would be repeated eight times.

EXAMPLE 3.1. Noel 13, lines 1-2, danced as a *pavane*.

Moderne modified	¢ ♩	♪ ♪	♩	♩	♩	♩
	A	la ve- nu-	e	de	No-	el
Arbeau's steps and	L	j	R			j
step-units	*simple* on left			*simple* on right		

Moderne modified	¢ ♩	♪ ♪	♩	♩	♩	♩	♩
	Cha-	cun se	doibt	bien	res-	jo-	ir
Arbeau's steps and	L		R	L			j
step-units	*double* on left						

Rippert's noels having eight-measure strains and 16-measure stanzas are twice as long as the Coming of Christmas Noel 13, so the forward–backward pattern would be performed twice in each stanza (Noels 5, 10, and 11):

> Strain 1. Left ss d forward
> Repeat of strain 1. Right ss d backward (with smaller steps)
> Strain 2 (first half). Left ss d forward
> Strain 2 (second half). Right ss d backward (with smaller steps)

In the Grazing Noel 3 the forward–backward pattern would be performed once for the unrepeated first musical strain and twice for the unrepeated second strain.

---

12. Arbeau (1596), 29v; Evans/Sutton trans., 59.

The structure of William Browne's keyboard *Allemande* to a melody similar to that of Noel 14 exactly fits Arbeau's *pavane*. Some later versions would fit Arbeau's *allemande*.

The *Allemande*

The earliest choreography for an *allemande* is found in a short treatise on *basses dances* published in London in 1521,[13] and two more appear in Moderne's collection of *basses dances* of the 1530s or 40s. All these *allemandes* include the opening bow and four-part step-units of the *basse dance* (to be discussed), but Arbeau gives a far simpler version in his manual of 1588.

Arbeau's is the only 16th-century French choreography for the *allemande* that includes music.[14] He attributes the dance to the Germans and describes it as simple and rather sedate (*plaine de mediocre gravité*).[15] Couples in a line step forwards, and sometimes backwards, from one end of the hall to the other; then they turn together and go the other direction.[16]

The *allemande*'s three steps and a *grève* (g) are like the *branle de Bourgogne* except that all steps are the same size and taken in the forward or backward direction. This step-unit fits two measures (four beats) of Rippert's noels with the 2 sign.

Count 1. Take a step forward onto the left foot (L).
Count 2. Take a step forward onto the right (R).
Count 3. Take another step forward onto the left (L).
Count 4. Poise the right foot in the air as the weight remains on the left foot (g).

As usual, a step-unit begun on the left foot is followed by one begun on the right: LRLg—RLRg.

LRLg   line 1   4 counts (2 measures)
RLRg   line 2   4 counts (2 measures)

In Arbeau's *allemande*, two one-measure step-units, one on the left and one on the right, interrupt the pairs of two-measure units as the music requires. The one-measure units are similar to the *simple*:

Count 1. Take a step forward onto the left foot (L).
Count 2. Poise the right foot in the air as the weight remains on the left foot (g).

Pellegrin's 1718 version[17] of the 16th-century Burghers' Noel 6 can be danced to Arbeau's *allemande*. (This is Rippert's version if the syllable *Christ* is held for a half note and a dotted quarter rest added before the next line.) Daquin's c. 1740 version of the 17th-century Birth of God Noel 14 also fits Arbeau's *allemande* (see ex. 2.8c for the second strain). Arbeau's bar lines pair left and right step-units of the same kind.

---

13. Robert Coplande, *Here Followeth the Manner of Dancing Bace Dances after the Use of France and Other Places translated out of French in English by Robert Coplande*, appendix to *The Introductory to Write and to Pronounce French*, by Alexander Barclay (London, 1521). Coplande's choreography for *La allemande* is cited in Daniel Heartz, "The Basse Dance: Its Evolution circa 1450 to 1550," *Annales Musicologiques* (Neilly-sur-Seine: Société de Musique d'Autrefois) 6 (1958–63): 306.

14. Daniel Heartz, "Allemande," *New Grove Dictionary*, vol. 1, 276.

15. Arbeau (1596), 67r; Evans/Sutton trans., 125.

16. *Ibid.*, 67r; trans., 125.

17. Simon-Joseph Pellegrin, *Chants des noëls anciens* (Paris, 1718). Also in *Poésies chrétiennes contenant noëls nouveaux* (1706; 1st ed. 1701) as cited in Ernest Myrand, *Noëls anciens de la nouvelle-France*, 2nd ed. (Quebec: Typ. Laflamme & Proulx, 1907), 145.

LRLg RLRg | (first strain)
LRLg RLRg | Lg Rg | LRLg RLRg | (second strain)

The Triple-Meter *Basse dance*

During the 16th century the timbres of many noels were identified as *basses dances* or given specific *basse dance* choreographies.[18] The large collection of *basses dances* published probably by Jaques Moderne in Lyon in the late 1530s or early 1540s contains the steps for *A la venuë de Noel* (Noel 13), unfortunately without music.

The *basse dance* is the oldest dance Arbeau discusses, long out of date when he wrote his book.[19] It is first encountered at the French court in the mid-15th century as an extremely light, graceful, and very complicated processional dance, but by the mid-16th century it had evolved into a simpler, more earth-bound, yet still elegant dance of the *haute bourgeoisie*.[20] Even in Arbeau's description, the latest found from the 16th century (1588), this dance uses a greater variety of motions and a more complicated structure than the others.

Basse dance music exists in both duple and triple meter, but the dance was in triple meter from around 1525 or perhaps later.[21] Arbeau says that tunes in duple meter are changed to triple when danced as *basses dances*.[22] Lebègue's first variation of the Coming of Christmas Noel 13 may be typical of the triple-meter rhythms used (ex. 3.2).[23]

EXAMPLE 3.2. Lebègue's triple-meter variation (1685) of *A la venuë de Noel* (Noel 13).

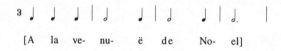

[A   la   ve-   nu-   ë   de   No-   el]

The earliest sources of *basse dance* choreographies are a 15th-century manuscript thought to have belonged to either Mary of Burgundy (died 1482), daughter of Charles the Bold and wife of Maximilian of Austria, or to her children (this manuscript is hereafter referred to as the Brussels manuscript);[24] and a printed dance manual, *L'Art et instruction de bien dancer*, published in Paris by Michel Toulouze around the 1480s.[25] The theoretical introductions of the two books are almost identical.

Basse dance choreographies are given as a series of letters, one for the opening *reverence* (R) and one for each of four step-units: *branle* (b, not to be confused with the dances called *branles*), pair of *simples* (ss), *double* (d), and *reprise* (r). Many choreographies include both a *basse dance* proper and a shorter *retour* (return, in which

18. See Block, vol. 2, under individual noels (e.g., nos. 111, 177, 186, 227, 266, 304, 316, 393, 427, 429, 437, 504, 518, 522, 556, 588).

19. Arbeau (1596), 24v; Evans/Sutton trans., 51.

20. Heartz, "The Basse Dance: Its Evolution," 287–8 and 325–6.

21. Evans/Sutton trans., p. 214, n. *a* for page 52.

22. Arbeau (1596), 37r–37v; Evans/Sutton trans., 75.

23. Nicolas Lebègue, *Troisieme livre d'orgue . . . et tous les noëls les plus connus . . . que l'on peut jouer sur l'orgue et le clavecin* (Paris, 1685), ed. Norbert Dufourq as *Noëls variés*, Orgue et Liturgie no. 16 (Paris: Éditions musicales de la Schola cantorum et de la Procure générale de musique, 1952), 9.

24. *Le manuscrit dit des basses dances de la Bibliothèque de Bourgogne* (Brussels, Bibliothèque royale, section des manuscrits, no. 9085); facs. reprint with introduction and transcription by Ernest Closson (Brussels: Société des bibliophiles et iconophiles de Belgique, 1912).

25. [Michel Toulouze], publ., *L'Art et instruction de bien dancer* (Paris, [1488?]); facs. reprint with bibliographical note by Victor Scholderer (London: The Royal College of Physicians of London, 1936). In Heartz, "The Basse Dance: Its Evolution," 288.

the dancers return to where they started).[26] The same step-units are used in the *basse dance* and *retour* but in a different sequence.

The Step-units of the Basse dance *and* Retour

For the *reverence*, the man bows to his partner and takes her hand (fig. 2). This would take four measures of Rippert's Noel 13 with the 3 sign and two with the 2 sign.

FIGURE 2. Arbeau's illustration of a couple performing a *reverence*.[27]

For the *branle*, the dancers stand in place with heels together and sway from side to side,[28] one motion to each musical measure. The Brussels and Toulouze sources explain that the *branle* is done by "wavering" (*bransler*) from one foot to the other. Daniel Heartz points out that Cotgrave's French–English dictionary of 1611 defines *bransler* as "to branle; totter; shake; swing; shog, wag, reele, stagger, wave, tremble or quake."[29]

<u>Count 1</u>. Turn the body gently to the left.
<u>Count 2</u>. Turn the body gently to the right.
<u>Count 3</u>. Turn the body gently to the left.
<u>Count 4</u>. Turn the body gently to the right.

For the *simples*, the dancers take one step to each count, one *simple* to every two counts, and one pair of *simples* to every two measures with the two sign and four measures with the 3 sign. The Brussels and Toulouze sources say that dancers perform either the second or both steps of the *simple* while "raising the body" (rising on the toes), but Arbeau's bourgeois dancers stay flat on their feet.[30]

For the *double*, the Brussels and Toulouze sources say that all four motions are performed in raising the body.[31] Again Arbeau's less elegant dancers walk on the soles of their feet.

For the *reprise*, the Brussels and Toulouze sources have dancers rise on tip-toe as they step back with the left foot and then bring the right foot back to join it.[32] Each motion takes two counts, so that the whole step-unit covers the four counts of the other step-units. Arbeau's *reprise* is quite different and not clearly explained: dancers stand in place but

---

26. In Arbeau's choreographies a *congé* (c) marks the end of both *basse dance* and *retour*. It is performed without music as the galant bows to the damsel, still holding her hand. Arbeau (1596), 26r; Evans/Sutton trans., 53–4.
27. Arbeau (1596), 40v; Evans/Sutton trans., 80.
28. *Ibid.*, 27r; trans., 55.
29. Heartz, "The Basse Dance: Its Evolution," 290.
30. *Ibid.*, 289.
31. *Ibid.*
32. *Ibid.*.

move their knees, feet, or toes a little (*remuent un peu*), as if shivering (*fremioient*).[33] In which direction and how far they move their knees, feet, or toes are not specified.

Brussels ms. and Toulouze print	Arbeau
<u>Counts 1–2</u>. Step backward with the left foot.	<u>Count 1</u>. Move the right toes.
	<u>Count 2</u>. Move the right toes again.
<u>Counts 3–4</u>. Bring the right foot back to join left.	<u>Count 3</u>. Move the left toes.
	<u>Count 4</u>. Move the right toes again.

Structures of the Basse dance *Choreographies*

The *basse dance* choreographies of the 15th century exhibit a complex structure of dance "measures" (*mesures*). By the 16th century a single choreography had become so popular that it was called the "common" *basse dance*.

Daniel Heartz points out that the dance *mesures* in the earlier treatises divided the *basse dance* into sequences of step-units.[34] After an initial R b (*reverence* and *branle*), all *mesures* began ss d (two *simples* and a *double*) and contained four to eleven units. In 15th-century choreographies, *mesures* of two contrasting lengths usually alternated. Heartz gives the following typical choreography, whose 34 step-units were grouped after the opening R b into four alternating *mesures* begun ss d (9 / 7 / 9 / 7):

R b / ss d d d ss r r r b / ss d ss r r r b / ss d d d ss r r r b / ss d ss r r r b /

Arbeau (1588) retains only the larger division into *basse dance* proper and *retour*.

Moderne (1730s or 1740s) clearly articulates the start of both *basse dance* proper and *retour* with a *reverence*. Arbeau starts only the *basse dance* proper with a *reverence* but closes it and the *retour* with a *congé* (c). For the *congé* the gentleman salutes the lady, takes her hand, and returns her to their starting place in order to begin again with the *retour* or another dance[35] (because the *congé* is not a step-unit and takes no time in Arbeau's tablature set to music, we relegate it to parentheses below).

In the common *basse dance* of the 16th century, 32 step-units are divided into a 20-unit *basse dance* proper and 12-unit *retour*. The step-units of the common choreography as given by Moderne with *mesures* and by Arbeau without them are:

basse dance proper (Moderne):	R b / ss d r d r b / ss d d d r d r b / ss d r b
basse dance proper (Arbeau):	R b ss d r d r b ss d d d r d r b ss d r b (c)
retour (Moderne):	R d r b / ss d d d r d r b
retour (Arbeau):	b d r b ss d d d r d r b (c)

The Four Step-units that Start All Basses dances

Although the sources cite many different *basse dance* choreographies, all begin with the same four step-units: R b ss d. The first stanza of the Coming of Christmas Noel 13, whether changed to triple meter or not, fits these first four units (ex. 3.3). After the bow of the *reverence*, one motion is made to each musical measure.

33. Arbeau (1596), 28r; Evans/Sutton trans., 56.
34. Heartz, "The Basse Dance: Its Evolution," 291–5 and 300–7.
35. Arbeau (1596), 26r; Evans/Sutton trans., 53-4.

EXAMPLE 3.3. Noel 13, Lebègue's variation in triple meter, danced to the first four step-units of the *basse dance*.

line 1	♩ [A	♩ la	♩ ve-	♩ nu-	♩ ë	♩ de	♩ No-	♩ el
step-unit 1	*reverence* (R)							

line 2	♩ Cha-	♩ cun	♩ se	♩ doit	♩ bien	♩. ré-	♪ ♩ joü-	♩. ir,
dance steps for	turn L			turn R		turn L		turn R
step-unit 2	*branle* (b)							

line 3	♩ Car	♩ c'est	♩ un	♩ tes-	♩ ta-	♩ ment	♩ nou-	♩. vel
dance steps for	step L			close		step R		close
step-unit 3	pair of *simples* (ss)							

line 4	♩ Que	♩ tout	♩ le	♩ mon-	♩ de	♩ doit	♩ te-	♩. nir.
dance steps for	step L			step R		step L		close
step-unit 4	*double* (d)							

Two adjustments must be made to dance Mary's Narrative Noel 9 to the first four step-units of the *basse dance*. First, as discussed in chapter 2, the music of Rippert's second strain must start the song, along with the old lyrics of Sergent, Oudot, and Ballard (first quatrain in ex. 3.4). Second, two dance motions must be made to each three-beat musical measure (the four motions of each step-unit made to two measures).

EXAMPLE 3.4. Rippert's Noel 9, sung to Oudot's lyrics and danced to the first four step-units of the 15th-century *basse dance*.

Rippert's 3/2 rhythm:	♩	♩.	♩ ♩ ♪	♩	♩	♩	♩.	♩ ♩ ♪	o
Oudot's lyrics:	Chan- tons		je vous en pri-	e	Par	ex-		al- ta- ti- on,	
	En l'hon-		neur de Ma- ri-	e	Plai-	ne		de grand re-nom.	

Four-beat step rhythm:		♩.	♩.	♩.	♩.		♩.	♩.	♩.	♩.	
(R / b)		bow		rise		/ turn L	turn R	turn L	turn R	/
(ss / d)		step L	close	step R	close	/ step L	step R	step L	close	/
Etc.										

Fitting the Basse dance *Sequences of Step-units to Noel Music*

If the first four step-units of the *basse dance*, R b ss d, are considered an introduction, the step-units of the common choreography can be construed in five segments that match the early poetic layouts of Noels 3, 7, 9, and 13 discussed in chapter 2. The first quatrain would be danced to the initial four step-units (first segment). The first two octaves would be danced to the rest of the *basse dance* proper (two eight-unit segments). The third octave and final quatrain would be danced to the *retour* (eight- and four-unit segments).

R b ss d // r d r b ss d d d / r d r b ss d r b // R (or b) d r b ss d d d / r d r b

The alignment of poetry and choreography in the Coming of Christmas Noel 13 fits Moderne's seven fully printed stanzas and an additional four lines of "Noel/noel/noel/ noel," indicated once after Moderne's seventh stanza (ex. 3.5).

EXAMPLE 3.5. Stanza 1 of Rippert's Noel 13, sung to Moderne's lyrics (first line of each stanza represents the whole stanza) and danced to *basse dance* proper and *retour*.

Introduction of *basse dance*

	1	*A la venue de Noel. . . .*	R b ss d
		(At the coming of Christmas)	

Rest *of basse dance* proper

	2	*Par son grand orgueil Lucifer. . . .*	r d r b
		(By his great pride, Lucifer)	
	3	*En une vierge s'en umbra. . . .*	ss d d d
		(And within a Virgin He cast his shadow)	
	4	*Apres ung bien petit de temps. . . .*	r d r b
		(After a very little time)	
	5	*A Dieu le vindrent presenter. . . .*	ss d r b
		(To God they came to present it	

Retour

	6	*La veirent le doulx Jesuchrist. . . .*	R (or b) d r b
		(There they saw sweet Jesus Christ)	
	7	*Bien apparut qu'il nous ayma. . . .*	ss d d d
		(It was clear that He loved us)	
	8	*Noel! Noel! Noel! Noel! . . .*	r d r b

The 32 step-units of the common *basse dance* and *retour* fit no version we found of Mary's Narrative Noel 9. Neither the quatrain and four octaves of the *Helas* chanson, the 43 quatrains of Sergent's noel (41 quatrains and final octave in Oudot), nor the 34 quatrains and final octave implied by Pellegrin's timbre (the version in our edition in Part II) matches the common structure. If either the *Helas* chanson or the early noel was performed as a *basse dance*, it was to one of the less common choreographies.

Two Triple-meter Dances with Fast Kicks

Arbeau's other triple-meter dances feature fast *grèves* or *pieds en l'air*, the *grève* being the higher kick. The quick kicks would articulate the opening quarter notes and following downbeat in every two measures of the Love of Mary Noel 7. This may explain why the noel developed its particular rhythm:

The fast kicks could express the fury of Noel 7's timbre, *Faulce trahison, Dieu te mauldie* (False treachery, God curse you) or the exuberance of the noel lyrics: joyous singing for the love of Mary.

The *Branle gay*

The *branle gay* is the triple-meter ring dance that Arbeau says usually follows the *branle double* and *branle simple* to open balls. The student with whom Arbeau converses throughout his treatise suggests this *branle* is called "gay" because one or the other foot is always in the air.[36] Each step-unit takes six counts: two measures of Rippert's music with the 3 sign.

The step-unit for the *branle gay* consists of four quick *pieds en l'air* followed by a pause. A bar line in the tablature concludes each step-unit. Dancers move always to the left (though the *pieds en l'air*, made toward the center of the circle, somewhat impede sideways progress). All step-units start with stepping onto the left foot.

>Count 1. Step onto the left foot while raising the right into the air (rp); step onto the right foot while raising the left into the air (lp); step onto the left foot while raising the right into the air (rp).
>Count 2. Step onto the right foot while raising the left into the air (lp); remain in this position for the rest of the count.

Each four-beat line of the Love of Mary Noel 7 would require two identical step-units:

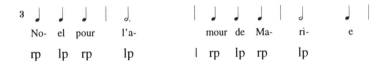

The *Galliard*

The *galliard*'s final leap would further enhance Noel 7's exuberance as the dancers leap for joy. A leap follows the four kicks in each step-unit of the *galliard*. The step-unit is named the *cinq pas* (five steps) for its five motions.

The *cinq pas* fill two measures of Rippert's music with the 3 sign (a bar line in Arbeau's tablatures concludes each step-unit). The first measure has three quick *grèves*, and the second has one *grève*, a *saut majeur* (large leap), and a *posture* (a landing with one foot in front of the other; ex. 3.6).[37] For the right posture, the right foot is forward; vice versa for the left (fig. 3).[38] Each four-measure line of Noel 7 would require two *cinq pas*. The first would begin on the left foot, with the right foot being kicked in the air; the second, vice versa.

---

36. *Ibid.*, 71v–72r; trans., 134.
37. *Ibid.*, 53r–53v ; trans., 100–1.
38. *Ibid.*, 47r; trans., 90.

FIGURE 3. Arbeau's right and left posture.

EXAMPLE 3.6. Arbeau's *cinq pas* for the *galliard*.

♩	♩	♩	♩		♩
R in air	L in air	R in air	L in air	leap	R posture

Matching 16th-century Noels to Dance Structures

To find the step-units that best fit the structure of a particular noel requires comparing the structures of music and dance. The summary given below includes repeats only with new texts. Those of Rippert's 16th-century noels that exhibit the musical structure are given in parentheses. Those in square brackets need some alteration to be danced.

With the 2 sign

(*Note:* If the piece starts at mid-measure, the barring will need to be displaced half a measure.)

- Noels with paired two-measure units have the structure of the *branle double* and *branle de Bourgogne*. (Noels 3, 5, 10, 11, 13, [15], and [16])
- Noels that consist solely of eight-measure periods, strains, or whole stanzas have the balanced structure of the *pavane*. (Noels 3, 5, 10, 11, 13, [15], and [16])
- Noels consisting of four- or eight-measure units with an occasional added two-measure unit have the looser structure of the *allemande*. (Noel [6])
- Noels with three-measure units have the structure of the *branle simple*. (Noel 12)
- Noels having units or irregular lengths are suitable for the mixed *branles*. (Noels 6, 15, and 16)

With the 3 sign

- Noels covering 16 or 32 measures fit the common *basse dance* and *retour*. (Noel 7)
- Noels that flow in two-measure units fit the *branle gay*. (Noel 7)
- Noels that flow in paired two-measure units fit the *galliard*. (Noel 7)

With the 3/2 sign

- Noels covering 16 measures fit the first four step-units of the *basse dance*. (Noel 9)

4

Performance of Noel Melodies

French singers sang noels and other *chansons populaires* in a way that imitated everyday speech. Numerous sources assert that French song was guided more by speech melodies and accents than by harmonic considerations, and the same sources declare that instrumentalists copied the style.[1] Speaking (not singing) noel lines, as in a rustic play, gives a variety of clues to musical performance. Between and across the regular beats of step-units, noel melodies flowed to the rather different rhythm of lyrics.

In this chapter we show how noel music and lyrics suggest tempo and affect (mood, feeling). We outline general principles on how noel lines and their word groups are set to music. We discuss the articulation unique to French poetry, as well as the contrary accents in many noels. We consider the articulation of eighth notes by flutists and singers, and the ornaments that simulate inflections of French speech.

Noel Tempo and Affect

The first indication of tempo comes from 16th-century step-units. Most noel melodies must be thought of in the four-beat units of the most common Renaissance dances (four half-note beats in Rippert's noels with the 2 sign; four dotted half-note beats with the 3 sign). Any beating of individual quarter, half, or dotted-half notes destroys the flow of dance and lyrics.

The second indication of tempo is the meter sign. The 2 and slashed C signs suggest a faster tempo than the C sign. The 3 indicates a quicker tempo than 3/2, and white notation calls for a brisker tempo than black (see app. 3, *Or nous dites Marie*).

The third indication of tempo is the spoken tidings of the particular lyrics. The words often pour out rapidly in excited joy: "Where are they going?" "Now tell us, Mary," "Let's sing, let's sing," "Alleluia." Rippert's quarter notes, set to the syllables of exhilarated speech, move very quickly. A tempo of about M.M. 80–90 to the half note may well express most lyrics with the 2 and 3/2 signs, though the Singing Noel 5 and the Burghers' Noel 6 might be spoken a little faster and Joseph's Noel 10 a little slower. Dotted half notes at about M.M. 40–54 may best express most lyrics with the 3 sign, many of which are tender in affect. Rippert marked Noels 4, 7, and 8 *Tendrement*, and tenderness is associated with slow speech. The Humble/Worldly Shepherdesses Noel 2 might be spoken somewhat more quickly.

All noels are performed rustically and simply, but the particular affect of a song depends on its mode, tempo, melody, rhythm, and lyrics. In Noel 1, the major mode, repeated pitches on quarter notes, and the opening question,"Where are these happy shepherds going, together side by side?" suggest happiness, equanimity, and comradeship, along with urgency and a fairly rapid tempo (ex. 4.1a). The shepherds' response, a gently rising and falling line and then a phrase suddenly in a higher range, projects first the shepherds' inner joy, "We are going to see Jesus Christ," and then their wonder that he was "born in a grotto" (ex. 4.1b).

In Noel 9, the marking *Très lentement* (Very slowly) suggests a quieter manner and more leisurely pace. Yet the mixed note values of the music, the melodic leaps of fifths

---

1. Patricia M. Ranum, personal correspondence, February 1996.

and fourths contrasted with repeated pitches, and the persistent request, "Now tell us, Mary," evoke the awesome excitement of the unfolding tale (ex. 4.2).

EXAMPLE 4.1. *Ou s'en vont ces gais bergers* (Noel 1). a. mm. 1–4. b. mm. 5–8.

[Où s'en vont ces gais ber - gers En- sem- ble côte à cô - te:]

[Nous al - lons voir Je - sus - Christ Né de - dans u - ne grot - te:]

EXAMPLE 4.2. *Or nous dites Marie* (Noel 9), mm. 1–2.

[Or nous di - tes Ma - ri - e]

Rippert sets his flute duets in D major and D minor. The noels in D major appear in C major or occasionally G major in other sources; but D major is an easy key for beginners on the transverse flute and parallels D minor, the usual key for the minor pieces. Marc-Antoine Charpentier called D major "joyous and warlike," C major "gay and warlike," and G major "sweetly joyous."[2] Joyous, gay, and sometimes sweetly joyous feelings are eminently suitable for the stories of happy shepherds (Noel 1), the very discreet new mother (Noel 2), inordinate joy (Noel 14), great joy on this day (Noel 6), joyful singing (Noels 3, 4, 5, 7, 15, and 16), and the unprecedented awakening (Noel 8). Charpentier called D minor "grave and devout," which describes the serious, reverent, and reflective accounts of Mary the Virgin (Noels 9, 10, and 11), the solemn day (Noel 12), and the new testament that all the world must embrace (Noel 13).

Musical Phrases from Noel Lines

Instrumentalists need to know the typical phrasing of the *chansons populaires,* even without lyrics to guide them. Lyrics are often lost or omitted and, in the case of the tender little airs for instruments by such composers as Marin Marais and François Couperin, probably never existed. The first two lines of a noel normally begin with identical, similar, or complementary music (table 2). Later lines tend to imitate the first two. The noel lyrics in this chapter are those used in our edition in Part II.

---

2. Marc-Antoine Charpentier, "Energie des modes," *Règles de composition* (Bibliothèque Nationale, Paris, ms. n.a. fr. 6355), f. 13–13v. In Patricia M. Ranum, "Do French Dance Songs Obey the Rules of Rhetoric?" *Fluting and Dancing: Articles and Reminiscences for Betty Bang Mather on her 65th Birthday,* ed. David Lasocki (New York: McGinnis & Marx, 1992), 121–2.

TABLE 2. First two lines of ten of Rippert's noels. Rhyming syllables underlined.

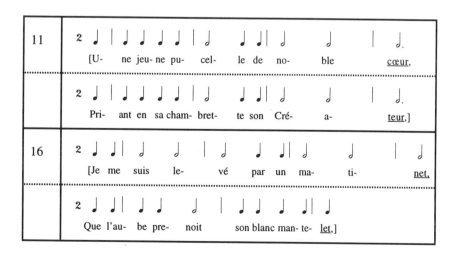

Length of Noel Lines

Most of Rippert's noels with the 2 and 3/2 signs cover two bars of music, and most with the 3 sign cover four bars (see table 2). The exceptions are the Young Virgin's Noel 11, with its doubly long lines for duple meter; the New Morning Noel 16, with a doubly long line followed by a compressed long line; the Humble/Worldly Shepherdesses' Noel 2 and the Endlessly Desiring Noel 4, which pair a line of almost four bars with one of slightly over two; and the Happy Shepherds' Noel 1 (see ex. 4.1), whose first line ends and second begins one quarter note early.

The number of syllables in a line governs the number of notes in a musical phrase: one note is normally used for each syllable.[3] Even the soft *e* of a feminine rhyme, though not counted as a separate syllable, has its own note. Some noels have the same number of syllables through all lines or pairs of lines. Others use the same number in the first strain, with some variation in the second.

The length of a line influences its expression. Lines of six to eight syllables are the most common and the most calm. The unexpected brevity of the first very short line in a song underscores its meaning: *Dis-moi pourquoi*, "Tell me why" (Noel 2). Later short lines may act as an intense afterthought: *Avecque moi*, "With me" (Noel 2). With very long lines, time seems to stretch out in leisure and tranquillity: *Une jeune pucelle de noble cœur*, "A young maiden of noble heart" (Noel 11).

Noel Rhymes

Late Baroque composers setting early noels to musical measures placed a bar line just before the first rhyming syllable so that it would fall on a downbeat (see table 2). They laid out the rest of the first line across the earlier measures and laid out subsequent lines across the later measures. Almost all later rhymes also fall on downbeats. Rhyming syllables are normally set to long notes that furnish repose.

The musical start of a line functions as the musical rhyme. Some noels start on a downbeat, some with a single upbeat, and some at mid-measure. The second line often "rhymes" musically with the first (begins with the same rhythm). A mid-measure start characterizes most noels with the 2 sign. A single upbeat note begins a few noels with the 2 and 3/2 signs. Downbeat starts initiate all Rippert's noels with the 3 sign and a few with the 2 sign.

A masculine rhyme is set to one note of music, a feminine rhyme to two (see the variety of rhythms in table 2). The soft *e* of the feminine ending typically falls from the pitch of the rhyming syllable, keeps that pitch, or rises a half step to the tonic. Only once, in the Endlessly Desiring Noel 4, does it rise a third as the word *complainte* cries in anguish.

Where the rhythm obscures the gender of the rhyme, the relative pitches of the notes in question may help. The gender of the first line in the Happy Shepherds' Noel 1 is musically ambiguous because the rhyming syllable (*-gers*) is set to a quarter note (see ex. 4.1). The constant quarter-note rhythm and repeated pitches might suggest a feminine rhyme for the first line and a mid-measure start for the second, to match the first. However, the same quarter notes in the third and fifth lines leap up a fifth and then an octave (mm. 6 and 10), which would evoke a shrill scream in a feminine ending. Because the rhyme pairs of a song's lyrics and music tend to be repeated, this first line can be expected to be masculine.

---

3. In the few instances where Rippert gives two notes, he almost always slurs them together, which shows they represent a single syllable. In our edition we dot two such slurs that Rippert evidently forgot.

Word Groups within Noel Lines

The grouping of syllables within each noel line is not nearly as predictable as the line length and rhyme. The length of the word groups in a song and its timbre are seldom the same, and later stanzas rarely match the first. Nevertheless, an understanding of the characteristics and tendencies of French word grouping is essential for inflecting French lines properly.

Word groups join syllables by their grammatical identities, though French speakers recognize them by their lengthened final syllables (discussed below). We use six rules to determine the scansion. (1) A real or implied punctuation mark separates one unit from the next. (2) An exclamation or verbal command is set off from what follows. (3) A modifying phrase (usually introduced by a preposition or relative pronoun) is separated from what it modifies. (4) A non-pronoun subject or non-pronoun direct or indirect object is separated from its verb. (5) A noun is separated from its adjective, and a verb from its adverb, when the adjective or adverb immediately follows its noun or verb. (6) A conjunction belongs with the noun or the verb following.

Word groups embrace one to six syllables; most have three or four. The shortest and longest groups are the most intense.[4] A short word group comes emphatically like an exclamation or command and highlights a word or concept: *Né* (Born: Noel 1); *Quoi!* (What!: Noel 2); *Dis-moi* (Tell me: Noel 2); and *No-el* (Noel 7). A five- or six-syllable group sustains the thought, ending on the key idea which seems to take forever to appear: *le pe-tit nou-veau né* (the little newborn: Noel 1); *Ma-cu-la-ti-on* (Sin: Noel 5); *U-ne jeu-ne pu-cel-le* (A young virgin: Noel 11). For readers not well acquainted with French, appendix 4 gives the scansion for the first stanzas of all Rippert's noels, along with almost word-by-word translations.

The final syllable of a word group receives the most stress and normally falls on a downbeat, especially in the first line of a song. In songs with the 2 or 3/2 signs that start with one or two upbeat syllables, the end of the first group is expected on the first downbeat. In songs with the 3 sign, it is expected on the second downbeat. Later lines in a song are purposely more varied.

The scansion in the first line of many noels, however, is irregular, even where the timbre is regular. The irregularity heightens the expression. The end syllables of the following four noel timbres fall normally, but those of the corresponding noel lines do not (end syllables are underlined, a diagonal slash indicates the end of a syllable group, and a vertical stroke represents a bar line).

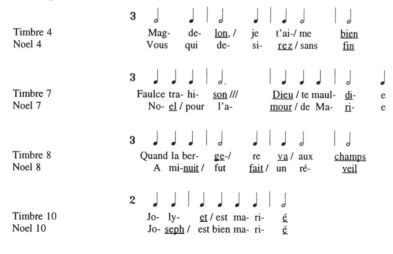

---

4. Ranum, personal correspondence, January 1995.

A soft *e* within a line, being unstressed, rarely ends a word group. Instead it normally flows into the next group, where it is treated as the first and shortest syllable. The first line of the Grazing Noel 3, which has no known timbre, is an exception. Its syllables would be spoken *Lais-sez paî- / tre vos bê-tes* (Let gra- / ze your flocks). But set to music, the ending *-tre* falls on a long note, on a beat, and is trilled, suggesting it concludes its group with a kind of internal rhyme: *Lais-sez paî-tre / vos bê-tes.*[5] In noels dating from the 16th-century, even the rhyming syllable may fall at mid-measure:

Noel 3, lines 1 and 2
Lais- | sez <u>paî</u>-tre / vos | <u>bê</u>-tes,
Pas- | tou-<u>reaux</u>, / par <u>monts</u> / | et par <u>vaux</u>

In 17th-century noels, the scansion of the first line is more likely to be normal, but great variety is still found in later lines. In the first stanza of Noel 1, only half the word groups end on downbeats, denying any sense of a regular meter. In the first stanza of Noel 2, all but one word group end on downbeats, making them fairly predictable:

Noel 1, first stanza	*Noel 2, first stanza*
Où s'en | <u>vont</u> / ces gais ber- | <u>gers</u>	Quoi, / ma voi- | <u>sine</u>, / és- | tu / fâ- | <u>ché</u>-e:
En-<u>sem</u>- | ble | <u>cô</u>-/ t(e) à <u>cô</u>- | te:	Dis- | <u>moi</u> / pour- | <u>quoi</u>?
Nous al- | lons <u>voir</u> / Jé-sus- | <u>Christ</u>	Veux-tu ve- | <u>nir</u> / <u>voir</u> /| l'ac-cou- | <u>ché</u>-e:
<u>Né</u> / de-dans | u-ne <u>grot</u>- | te:	A- | vec-que | <u>moi</u>?
Où est- | <u>il</u> / le pe-tit nou-veau | <u>né</u>,	C'est u-ne | <u>Da</u>-me /| fort dis- | <u>cre</u>-te,
Le ver-rons- | <u>nous</u> / en-<u>co</u>- | re?	Ce | m'a-t'on | <u>dit</u>,
	Qui nous a | pro-<u>duit</u> /| le Pro- | <u>phe</u>-te,
	Sou-| vent pré- | <u>dit</u>.

French Accentuation

Once a noel's lines and word groups have been identified, they must be enunciated as in French speech. French accentuation is based on principles quite different from English.

In English poetry, lines are often written as a series of repetitive metric feet. For example, the Christmas carol *Hark! the herald angels sing* is in trochaic tetrameter, meaning it has four groups of strong–weak feet (<u>Hark</u>! the / <u>herald</u> / <u>angels</u> / <u>sing</u>). The concept of feet is possible in the English language because words are made up of a series of stressed and unstressed syllables that remain constant no matter where the words occur in a group. Accenting the syllables is accomplished by pronouncing them more loudly, usually at a higher pitch than their neighbors. In *Hark! the herald angels sing,* the accented syllables of the poetry fall on the first and third quarter notes of the musical measure, its "good" notes. This makes the poetry fit the music well.

Most noel lines also fit four beats of music. But the accentuation of their syllables is not based on feet and meter, nor on loudness and pitch. French accentuation depends on the syllables' positions in word groups rather than in isolated words. French syllables are stressed by sustaining them, with no appreciable increase in loudness nor fluctuations in pitch.

---

5. Ranum, personal correspondence, February 1996.

The Relay

The crucial factor differentiating French from English accentuation is the "relay" at the end of all French word groups.[6] There the final syllables are gradually lengthened to allow the mind to rest momentarily before attempting to grasp the meaning of the next group (table 3). In units of only one syllable, that monosyllable forms the relay; in groups of two to four syllables, the final two syllables; in units of five or six syllables, the final two or three. Where a soft *e* falls on a relay syllable, the syllable before it is lengthened instead (*de no-ble cœur*, Noel 11). The final relay of a line normally straddles its bar line.

TABLE 3. Relay syllables in the first lines of ten of Rippert's noels. Relay syllables underlined.

Noel	First line
5	[Chan-tons/ je vous pri- e]
10	[Jo- seph / est bien ma-ri- é,]
3	[Lais-sez paî-tre / vos bê- tes,]
9	[Or nous di-tes / Ma-ri- e]

Noel	First line
7	[No-el / pour l'a- mour/ de Ma-ri- e]
8	[A mi-nuit / fut fait / un ré- veil]
2	[Quoi,/ ma voi-sine, / és- tu fâ-ché- e:]
4	[Vous / qui de-si-rez / sans fin,]

Noel	First line
11	[U- ne jeu-ne pu-cel- le / de no- ble cœur,]
16	[Je me suis le- vé / par un ma-ti- net,]

An interesting comparison can be made by first singing the "Hark!" carol in a rhythmically energetic, "English" way (accenting the syllables on the strong beats) and then in a dramatic "French" way (lingering gradually longer over the vowels and consonants in each underlined relay syllable): "Hark! / the her-ald an-gels / sing /// Glo-ry / to the new-born King, /// Peace / on earth / and mer-cy / mild, /// God / and sin-ners / re-con-ciled."

6. Joseph Pineau, *Le Mouvement rhythmique en français: principes et méthode d'analyse* (Paris: Klincksieck, 1979), 12 *et passim*. In Patricia M. Ranum, "Les 'Caractères' des danses françaises," *Recherches sur la musique française classique* 23: 51–6; "A Fresh Look at French Wind Articulations," *American Recorder*, 33/4: 12–13; "Do French Dance Songs Obey the Rules of Rhetoric?"*Fluting and Dancing*, ed. David Lasocki (New York: McGinnis & Marx, 1988): 110–12.

Contrary Accents at Relays

Many noels have accents contrary to standard French pronunciation. The end syllables of relays may fall on quarter notes or eighth notes, and not on beats. The normally unstressed soft *e* may fall on a long value, even on a downbeat, and sometimes on a note as long as that for the relay syllable before it.

Irregular accents may have become more noticeable with the addition of bar lines where none were originally conceived. All Rippert's noels that begin with a single upbeat syllable come from the 15th or 16th century and are particularly surprising in their accents. The words *U-ne jeu-ne pu-cel-le* (Noel 11) seem soft, graceful, and lilting until a bar line precedes the first *-ne*: then the soft *e*'s on three of the four beats become extremely expressive: *U-* | *ne jeu-ne pu-* | *cel-le*. In the other three noels with single upbeats (Noels 3, 6, and 9), a soft *e* ends the first word group of several lines on a beat. Within the eight lines of the first stanza of Mary's Narrative Noel 9, only two word groups end on downbeats (*fit*, *J'é-tois*) and only in the repeated first strain do relays end on dotted quarters. The final stressed syllable (*paî-*) of the Grazing Noel 3's first relay falls oddly on an eighth note, and the feminine ending (*-tre*) on a dotted quarter. The Burghers' Noel 6 is even stranger: in the first strain of its 16th-century version, which starts *Les Bourgeoises de Chastre* (the townswomen of Chastre, instead of the townsmen, or burghers), seven soft *e*'s fall on dotted quarter notes.[7]

Many soft *e*'s fall on beats in the 15th- and 16th-century noels having female subjects: Mary's Narrative Noel 9, the Young Virgin's Noel 11, and the Townswomen's early Noel 6. The 17th-century Humble/Worldly Shepherdesses' Noel 2, however, uses many feminine words but avoids placing their soft *e*'s on beats.

Woodwind Articulation of Unslurred Eighth Notes

In 1707 Jacques Hotteterre instructed beginning flute, recorder, and oboe players on the tonguing of eighth notes with the 2 and 3 signs. He recommended the syllables *tu* and *ru* be alternated and the odd-numbered ones in a bar played slightly longer than the even-numbered ones.[8] Vocal treatises of the period instead emphasize the importance of making the notes conform to speech patterns, and song lyrics confirm that a simple long–short or short–long performance of eighth notes is rarely appropriate (ex. 4.3).[9]

EXAMPLE 4.3. Noel 1, m. 9. Run of eighth notes.

[Où est - il / le pe- tit nou- veau né,]

7. The many soft *e*'s on beats in the early version of Noel 6 (see Sergent and Oudot) led most late Baroque sources to alter the first two lines. Ballard (1704) got rid of three errant *e*'s by changing the old *Les bour-geoi-ses de Chas- tres Et de Mont- le Hé-ry* to *Tous les bour- geois de Châ- tre Et ceux de Mont l'he- ry*. Rippert uses Ballard's first line as his title. We use Ballard's first two lines in our edition in Part II.

8. Jacques Hotteterre, *Principes de la flute traversiere, ou flute d'allemagne, de la flute a bec, ou flute douce, et du hautbois* (Paris, 1707). Facsimile of [1710] Amsterdam ed. with German translation by H. J. Hellwig (Kassel: Bärenreiter, 1941), 21–6. English translation by David Lasocki as *Principles of the Flute, Recorder and Oboe* (London: Barrie & Rockliff; New York: Praeger, 1968), 59–62. English translation by Paul Marshall Douglas as *Rudiments of the Flute, Recorder and Oboe* (New York: Dover, 1968), 36–41.

9. See Patricia M. Ranum, "*Tu-Ru-Tu* and *Tu-Ru-Tu-Tu*: Toward an Understanding of Hotteterre's Tonguing Syllables," *The Recorder in the 17th Century: Proceedings of the International Recorder Symposium Utrecht 1993*, ed. David Lasocki (Utrecht: STIMU [Stichting voor Muziekhistorische Uitvoeringspraktijk], 1995). We thank Patricia M. Ranum and David Lasocki for making a pre-publication copy of this article available to us.

Hotteterre neglects to prescribe syllables for a dotted-quarter–eighth figure with the 2 or 3/2 sign, or at the end of a bar with the 3 sign. Lyrics, however, show that a single eighth is long or short depending on its position in the word group. Modern players are often taught to "double-dot" or "over-dot" such figures, but the diversity of syllables on these notes in noels suggests a generally variable and "under-dotted" performance.

Several unslurred eighth notes follow one another in only three of Rippert's noels. In the 16th-century Noel 13 and 17th-century Noel 14 a pair of eighth notes falls among quarters. Hotteterre says that such a pair may be articulated *tu ru*. Three of the four lines of the Coming of Christmas Noel 13 begin with a four-syllable group composed of a quarter note, two eighths, and a following downbeat. The second eighth (third syllable) would be lengthened to start the first relay: *tu tu ru | tu*. Each of these three relays in Noel 13 begins with a continuous consonant (discussed below) that can be started early:

In the Birth of God Noel 14, five short lines begin with a three-syllable group composed of two eighth notes and a quarter. In three of these lines, the second eighth (second syllable) begins the relay with a continuous consonant that can be started early: *tu ru tu*.

In the other two short lines in Noel 14, a soft *e* falls on the second eighth, so that the previous syllable is lengthened instead: *Et ne frit*. Comparable woodwind articulations might be *tu te ru* or *tu re tu*, the syllable *te* simulating the soft *e*.

Hotteterre recommends alternating the syllables *tu* and *ru* for an unequal number of eighth notes until a downbeat long note: *tu ru tu ru tu | tu*. In the string of eighths in the Happy Shepherds' Noel 1 (see ex. 4.3), the final three would be lengthened for the relay. Patricia Ranum finds similar situations for most eighth-note runs in French songs and advises players to concern themselves more with the gradual lengthening of the last three syllables than with the relative inequality of the first three.[10]

Noel Ornaments

Ornaments in noels articulate the beats for dancers, stress the relays of singers, and imitate vocal inflections. In *Doubles* they decorate the whole noel melody.

To aid projection and enhance their message, French Baroque preachers, lawyers, actors, and opera singers sustained vowels and emphasized initial consonants at relays. Instantaneous consonants like *b, d, g, k, p, qu,* and *t* were pronounced more crisply than usual, making an abrupt articulation silence. Continous consonant and consonant groups like *f, l, m, n, r, v, ch, gn, gr,* and *tr* were started slowly and gently and sustained longer than usual. The vowel set to music begins at the notated start of the note; the consonant, whether instantaneous or continuous, and whether emphasized or not, begins early.[11] A large majority of the relays in table 3 begin with continuous consonants that could be given extra length. To what extent the rustic folk who sang noels used the intensified expression of the pulpit, law court, and theatre is not known, but 18th-century instrumentalists imitated these lengthenings with ornaments.

---

10. Ranum, personal correspondence, January 1995.
11. Ranum, personal correspondence, February 1995.

The instrumental arrangements of noels, even without lyrics, agree remarkably on the position of ornaments on the upbeat and often the downbeat syllables at most relays, above all at the end of a line. The ornaments may be trills, *pincés* (mordents), one- or two-note graces before or after the main note, or slurred quick notes. Typical is the second strain of the Endlessly Desiring Noel 4, whose melodies, rhythms, and even phrase lengths differ among 18th-century arrangements (marked with circles, brackets, and boxes in ex. 4.4). Yet an ornament stresses the penultimate syllable of almost all six-measure phrases: *chan-ter*, *les jours*, *se-cours*. Even Raison, who decorates most beats in bagpipes fashion for dancers, abandons that pattern to strengthen by length the mid-measure soft *e* of the last relay: *se-cours*.

EXAMPLE 4.4. Five versions of Noel 4, strain 2. Variant pitches circled; variant rhythms bracketed; supplementary measures boxed; relay syllables underlined. a. Ballard (1704/12). b. Raison, *Second Livre d'Orgue* [1714]. c. Dandrieu, *Noëls, O filii* [?1721–33]. d. Rippert (1725). e. Lalande, *Symphonie des Noëls,* no. 12 (1727).

Trills and Pincés

The + sign may stand for a trill or a *pincé*. If approached from above, a trill is meant; if from below, perhaps a *pincé*.

Bagpipers, who by the nature of their instruments cannot separate notes, need such ornaments on the first of a pair of continuously slurred eighth notes to make the beats clear for dancers. Raison uses a trill or *pincé* on almost every beat in his organ settings of noels (see ex. 4.4b). Rippert's second flutist trills many downbeats.

Trills and *pincés* often give weight to the upbeat syllables at relays. In pieces with and without lyrics, a trill or *pincé* goes hand in hand with a syllable that is "long," and a "long" syllable is normally part of a relay.[12]

Of the 14 trills in the two flute parts of Rippert's Noel 1 (some of which may be performed as *pincés*), all but those on the expressive words *gais* and *Jesus* appear at relays. The trilled *-gers* of *ber-gers* highlights the downbeat, gives a feeling of length to the unusually short note on the final relay syllable, and sets up the early entrance of the second line. The first trill on the final *côte* points to the rhyme, which would normally fall on the downbeat; the second trill provides the necessary sense of length to the soft *e* on the downbeat. The second flute's trills in the first strain initiate the four-beat dance rhythms; in the second strain, they point up three downbeat relays and the final upbeat relay.

Trills and *pincés* make happy, agitated, and beautiful sounds. The trilled *gais* and *Jesus* in Noel 1 express the shepherds' exhilaration (see ex. 4.1). In one line of Noel 3 (ex. 4.5) a trill on *beau* (beautiful) makes the nightingale's song even more lovely, and a trill and *pincé* on the first and last syllables of *ré-son-neau* (resonant) make it even more sonorous and vibrant.

EXAMPLE 4.5. Noel 3, mm. 16–17.

[Si haut,   si   beau,   si   ré - son - neau]

Most tutors of the early eighteenth century teach that trills begin on the beat and with the upper auxiliary. In these simple vocal melodies passed down from earlier times, a start before the beat and with the principal note may often sound better. In example 4.5, the trill on *beau* might begin on the beat, with or without a quick upper auxiliary to give the bite of the instantaneous consonant. Both ornaments on the word *résonneau* might start before the beat to suggest elongated consonants. Most trills and *pincés* in these songs sound best when shaken only once or twice at the beginning of the ornamented note.

One-note Graces before the Main Note

The one-note grace makes a gracious emphasis that precedes or follows its main note. When it precedes the main note, it is performed before or on the beat and briskly, caressingly, or somewhere in between. Ranum finds that the single grace slurred into a note is almost always set to a syllable begun with a sustainable consonant.[13] If before the beat, it brings to mind the gentle humming and lengthening of a long consonant; if on

---

12. Ranum, personal correspondence, January 1996.
13. Ranum, personal correspondence, January 1995.

the beat and quick, the sharp bite of an instantaneous one. In Noel 3 a one-note grace anticipates and makes longer and more songlike the final syllable of *ros-si-gnol* (nightingale, m. 12). In the second strain of Noel 7, a one-note grace notated on the beat extends the start of the life-giving *vie* (ex. 4.6).

EXAMPLE 4.6. Noel 7, mm. 9–12.

[Quand   elle   por - ta   le   fruit   de   vi - e]

Where a one-note grace fills the interval of a falling third that ends on a weak part of the beat, it is performed gracefully and usually before the note. In the *Double* of Noel 1 (flute 2, m. 4), the ornament expresses the gaiety and togetherness of the shepherds. In Noel 11, line 4, it savors the mystery described; for full effect, the *r* of *mystere* might be started before and sustained across the beat (ex. 4.7).

EXAMPLE 4.7. Noel 11, mm. 9-10.

[Lui   con - ta   le   my - ste - re]

One- or Two-note Graces after the Main Note

A one-note grace slurred to the end of a note sustains the vowel as an intensification, or *accent*. The ornament sometimes anticipates the pitch of the final note of the phrase. In Noel 1 (ex. 4.8), this grace slides like a caress to the final syllables *grotte* (grotto) and *encore* (yet). In Noel 4 (ex. 4.9) it prolongs the trilled first syllable in singing style: *chaan-ter* (sing). In Noel 9 (ex. 4.10), it simulates a lilt of the voice in recalling a happy time and place: *Ga-lilée*, *re-gion*, *en-fermée*.[14] The double grace in Noel 8 extends the bell-like trilled first syllable of "awakening": *rée-veil* and leads to the final note of the phrase (ex. 4.11).[15]

---

14. Ranum suggests that, with important nasalized vowels such as the first syllables of *chanter* and *enfermée*, the pure vowel be sung throughout the main note and nasalized only with the one-note grace. Personal correspondence, March 1994.

15. For more on the performance of French ornaments that are notated as signs, see Frederick Neumann, *Ornamentation in Baroque and Post-Baroque Music* (Princeton University Press, 1978); Betty Bang Mather, *Interpretation of French Music from 1675 to 1775* (New York: McGinnis & Marx, 1973); and Mather and Dean Karns, *Dance Rhythms of the French Baroque* (Bloomington: Indiana University Press, 1988), Chapter 15.

EXAMPLE 4.8. Noel 1, mm. 7–8 and 11–12. a. line 4. b. line 6.

[Né de - dans u - ne grot - te:]   [Le ver - rons - nous en - co - re?]

EXAMPLE 4.9. Noel 4, mm. 5–8.

[Oü - ir chan - ter]

EXAMPLE 4.10. Noel 9, mm. 5–10.

[J'é - tois en Ga - li - lé - e Plai - san - te re - gi -

on, En ma chambre en - fer - mé - e,]

EXAMPLE 4.11. Noel 8, mm. 1–4.

[A mi - nuit fut fait un ré - veil]

Slurred Pairs of Eighths

Eighth notes slurred in pairs, one syllable to a pair, appear rarely in Rippert's noels (except in *Doubles*). Lyrics set to slurred eighths normally speak soft and tender thoughts.[16] This decoration caresses the syllable with its sliding pitch: Noel 10, *de Jes-sé* and *ma-ri-é*; Noel 14, *n'ap-por-tait*; and Noel 16, *man-te-let*. The doubled pairs in Noels 10 and 16 introduce the relay of their lines.

The noel *Doubles* by Rippert and many organists suggest the running eighth notes of bagpipers, who would group the notes in unequal pairs under their continuous slur to point up the underlying rhythm for dancers. The first and third eighth notes of each beat would be played in time, the second late, and the fourth early (ex. 4.12). The first and fourth would be longer than notated to bring out the dance rhythm and the relay syllables. The second and third would be shorter.

---

16. Ranum, personal correspondence, January 1996.

EXAMPLE 4.12. Noel 14, *Double*, mm. 10–14).

[Et <u>no</u>, <u>no</u>, / et <u>ne</u> <u>frit</u>, Et <u>n'of</u> - frit / sans ces - se]

Bar Lines as Guides for Instrumentalists' Phrasing

In this chapter we have related the lyrics of Rippert's noels to his bar lines, whereas in chapters 2 and 3 we showed that these bar lines disagree with early dance steps. Actually, whether Noel 13 is barred *A la ve-nu-ë | de No-el* or *A la ve- | nu-ë de No- | el* does not affect how the lyrics are sung, which is *A la ve-nu- / ë de No-el*. French lines and word groups flow toward their relays regardless of bar lines. Thus the transition from the old *chansons à danser* to the 18th-century ornamented arrangements for flute and organ is not as great as might appear. These simple, pastoral, and long-loved songs retain the tempos, affects, phrasing, and articulation of French shepherds' dance and speech.

For instrumentalists having no lyrics for guidance, bar lines are useful markers. They help define the overall structure and identify the masculine and feminine endings. They aid in locating the two-measure lines in noels with the 2 and 3/2 signs, which often overlap bar lines. They help identify the four-measure lines in noels with the 3 sign, which begin on downbeats. They point out where most relays would be and suggest the function and performance of most ornaments.

Instrumentalists can study Rippert's noels in Part II and the English translations and scansions of first stanzas in appendix 4 to find to what extent these *chansons populaires* confirm the general principles laid down in this chapter. They can investigate where, how, and why deviations occur. From the ornaments and *Doubles* they can learn to decorate similar little airs in instrumental music. If they can memorize at least one French stanza, they can dance and sing to the music as did the shepherds and shepherdesses in many noel lyrics.

5

Flutes, Shepherds, Angels, and Song

Arrangements of *chansons populaires* for flutes or recorders were fairly common in the early 18th century, though Rippert's are the only such noel arrangements we found. Jane Bowers shows that flutes had long been connected with Christmas; as instruments of shepherds and angels they figured in numerous Christmas paintings and illustrations.[1] Bowers and more recently John Anderies have also collected considerable pictorial, literary, and musical evidence that flutes performed vocal music from the early 15th through the early 18th centuries.[2] Anderies documents the exceptional ability of the conical, one-keyed, transverse, wooden flute of the late 17th and early 18th centuries to imitate the inflections of impassioned speech. The simple vocal airs, including Rippert's noels, were considered excellent practice material for 18th-century flutists, and Rippert's duet arrangements were modeled on vocal duets of the period. Most of the information and primary quotations in this chapter were collected by Bowers and Anderies.

The 14th through 16th Centuries

In the late 14th century, the transverse flute had two uses: as a *doulz instrument* (soft instrument) for intimate music and, with the *tabour* (drum), for military music.[3] It was as a soft instrument that it is seen accompanying singers in early illustrations. Angels play various instruments, including two transverse flutes, in the large border surrounding a miniature depicting the "Coronation of the Virgin" in Jean de Berry's *Petites Heures* of the late 14th century.[4] In his *Belles Heures* of the early 15th century, a transverse flute, harp, timpani, lute, bowed fiddle, and portatif appear in the border of a miniature of the "Annunciation."[5] The same instruments are held by angels in the frontispiece of a *Bible moralisée* of about 1411.[6] Two other early 15th-century miniatures depicting transverse flutes illustrate shepherds mourning the death of Daphnis.[7]

During the rest of the 15th century, artistic depictions of the transverse flute disappear in Europe, but Bowers has found some French references to *flahutes* or *fleutes,* which may include the transverse instrument. Between 1409 and 1411 a Christmas celebration for King Charles VI featured the soft *flahutes, tambourins, chalemies, harpes, vielles,* and

---

1. Jane M. Bowers, "French Flute School from 1700 to 1760," Ph.D. diss. (University of California, Berkeley, 1971); "New Light on the Development of the Transverse Flute between about 1650 and about 1770," *Journal of the American Musical Instrument Society* 3 (1977): 5–56, and "'Flaüste traverseinne' and 'Flûte d'Allemagne': The Flute in France from the Late Middle Ages up through 1702," *Recherches sur la musique française classique* 19 (1979): 7–50.

2. John Anderies, "Chansons, Airs & Brunettes: The Practice of Playing French Vocal Music on the Transverse Flute," transcript of Masters degree lecture-recital (Case Western Reserve University, 1993), and "Vocal Music for the Transverse Flute," *Traverso* 6, no. 3 (July 1994): 1–3. Reproductions of various pictures of the transverse flute with shepherds, angels, the muses, or amorous song are shown in Bowers, "French Flute School" and "New Light," and in Anderies, "Chansons." Footnotes in Bowers, "Flaüste traverseinne" and "New Light" show where to find reproductions of the pictures she describes but does not reproduce.

3. Bowers, "Flaüste traverseinne," 13–14.

4. Paris, Bibliothèque nationale, ms. latin 18014, f. 48v. Bowers, "Flaüste traverseinne," 14–15, dates the *Petites Heures* as no later than 1388.

5. Bibliothèque nationale, ms. fr. 166, f. 30. Bowers, "Flaüste traverseinne," 15, dates the *Bible moralisée* between 1408 and 1413.

6. Located at The Cloisters, New York. Bowers, "Flaüste traverseinne," 15, dates the *Belles Heures* between 1408 and 1413.

7. These are attributed to the Roman Texts and the Luçon Workshops. See Millard Meiss, *The Limbourgs and Their Contemporaries*, 2 vols. (New York: George Braziller, The Pierpont Morgan Library, 1974), plates 235 and 237, Plate Volume. In Bowers, "Flaüste traverseinne," 15–16.

bebdons as well as the loud *trompettes* and *clarions.*[8] At a banquet in Lille in 1454, four of the 28 minstrels played *moult melodieusement* (very melodiously) on flutes.[9] At a marriage banquet in 1468 for Charles the Bold of Burgundy and Margaret of York, four musicians dressed as wolves played a *chanson* on four flutes.[10]

Evidence of the transverse flute reappears and the instrument rises to prominence by the 1530s,[11] the decade that produced our first surviving publications of noels with music, numerous collections of noel texts, and a collection of choreographies for simple chansons, among them *A la venuë de Noel* (see chap. 3). The Parisian printer Pierre Attaignant published the first music for flute during this decade. Sometime between 1531 and 1535, he printed 44 *chansons en duo*, intended principally for singers but described also as *delectable aux fleustes* (delectable on flutes);[12] unfortunately, these duets have not survived.[13] In 1533, he printed two volumes of *chansons* in four parts, some of which are marked as suitable for the transverse flute and some for the recorder.[14]

Various 16th-century paintings and illustrations show a transverse flutist playing *chansons populaires* with a singer and lutenist. In three much-reproduced paintings with similar subjects said to be by the Master of the Female Half-lengths, three ladies perform Claudin de Sermisy's *Jouissance vous donneray* (I will give you joy).[15] (Arbeau used this song to demonstrate the common *basse dance* discussed in chap. 3.[16]) One lady sings and two perform on transverse flute and lute. In an anonymous painting, also with multiple versions, two ladies play on flute and lute another *chanson* by Claudin de Sermisy, *Au pres de vous* (Close to you); a gentleman between the ladies points to the music, looks deeply into the face of the flutist, touches his right shoulder to her left, and with his left arm encircles both shoulders of the lutenist.[17] Two metal-block illustrations for Giovanni Boccaccio's *Decameron* in French translation (Paris, 1545) show a lady lutenist and gentleman flutist on the left, along with two singing ladies, a flutist, lutenist, and gambist on the right, performing what was probably music to accompany a *branle*, followed by *chansonettes* (both in the accompanying text).[18] Besides the flute-playing angels in 14th-century miniatures, the instrument appears in 16th-century concerts of angels, as in an *Adoration des bergers* (Adoration of the Shepherds) attributed to Jean de Gourmont, who was active in Paris and Lyon between 1506 and 1551.[19]

---

8. André Pirro, *La musique à Paris sous le règne de Charles VI (1380–1422)* (Strasbourg: Heitz & Cⁱⁱ, 1930), 27–9. In Bowers, "Flaüste traverseinne," 16.

9. Jeanne Marix, *Histoire de la musique et des musiciens de la cour de Bourgogne sous le règne de Philippe le Bon (1420–67)* (Strasbourg: Heitz & Cie, 1939), 37–43. In Bowers, "Flaüste traverseinne," 16.

10. *Mémoires d'Olivier de La Marche*, ed. Henri Beaune and J. d'Arbaumont, vol. 3 (Paris: Librairie Renouard, 1885), 151–4. In Bowers, "Flaüste traverseinne," 16–17.

11. Bowers, "Flaüste traverseinne," 7, 19–26.

12. Pierre Attaignant, publ. *Quarante et quatre chansons à deux, ou duo, chose delectable aux fleustes* (Paris, c. 1530–35).

13. For more information see Daniel Heartz, "*Au pres de vous*: Claudin's Chanson and the Commerce of Publishers' Arrangements," *Journal of the American Musicological Society* 24 (1971): 196. In Bowers, "Flaüste traverseinne," 20.

14. *Chansons musicales a quatre parties desquelles les plus convenables a la fleuste dallemânt sont signees en la table cy dessoubz escripte par a. et a la fleuste a neuf trous par b. et pour les deux fleustes sont signees par a. b.* and *Vingt et sept chansons musicales a quatre parties desquelles les plus convenables a la fleuste dallement sont signees en la table cy dessoubz escripte par a. et a la fleuste a neuf trous par b. et pour les deux par a. b.* Bowers, "Flaüste traverseinne," 19.

15. All three paintings depict the same basic scene. Anderies, "Chansons," 5, notes that a fourth painting by the same artist is very similar, but the tune being played bears no resemblance to *Jouissance vous donneray.* Bowers, "Flaüste traverseinne," 23, says that the version of the painting held by the Harrach Gallery (Vienna, Austria) is reprinted in Max Sauerlandt, *Die Musik in fünf Jahrhunderten der Europäischen Malerei* (Leipzig: Langewiesche, 1922), 19, and in Raymond Meylan, *La Flûte* (Lausanne: Payot, 1974), 83 [translated into German by Ilse Krämer and Raymond Meylan as *Die Flöte* (Bern and Stuttgart: Hallwag Verlag, 1974); translated from German into English by Alfred Clayton as *The Flute* (Portland, Oregon: Amadeus Press, 1988)]. The version in the Hermitage Museum (Petersburg, Russia) is reprinted in Georg Hirth, *Die Musik in der Malerei* (Munich: G. Hirth, 1924), plate 28. Although the paintings have commonly been attributed to the Flemish Master of the Half-lengths, Daniel Heartz, "Mary Magdalen, Lutenist," *Journal of the Lute Society of America* 5 (1972): 52–67, gives evidence of Parisian origin.

16. Thoinot Arbeau, *Orchesography,* 2nd ed. (Lengres, 1589), 33v–37r; Evans/Sutton trans., 67–74.

17. Heartz, "*Au pres de vous,*" 214; Bowers, "Flaüste traverseinne," 24; Anderies, "Chansons," 7.

18. Heartz, "*Au pres de vous,*" 219; Bowers, "Flaüste traverseinne," 24; Anderies, "Chansons," 8. The translation was published in Paris in 1545.

19. Bowers, "Flaüste traverseinne," 25. This painting is at the Louvre.

The 17th and Early 18th Centuries

Marin Mersenne's book on instruments, published in Paris in 1636, includes a four-part *Air de cour pour les flustes d'allemand*.[20] *Airs de cour* are strophic songs for four or five voices or for a single voice with lute. Anderies points out they were written by the most respected composers to entertain the king, chiefly during the reign of Louis XIII (1610–1643).[21] The air arranged for transverse flutes in Mersenne is *Sus, sus, sus, bergers et bergerettes* (Come, come, come, shepherds and shepherdesses). This song first appeared in 1620 by Pierre Guédron but Mersenne attributes it to Henry le Jeune, who may be the arranger.[22]

In paintings of the 17th century, the transverse flute participates in concerts of angels, muses, and lovers. Charles Le Brun's *Adoration des bergers* (1689) shows angel musicians playing the harp, cymbals, viol, and transverse flute.[23] In two paintings from the mid-17th century, Euterpe, the muse of lyric poetry (poetry suitable to be sung with a lyre), holds or plays a transverse flute.[24] In Robert Bonnart's engraving entitled *Simphonie du tympanum, du luth, et de la flûte d'allemagne* (Symphony of the tympanum, lute, and German [transverse] flute), probably of the 1690s, a lady and two gentlemen play together. A quatrain below the picture commends careful music-making made sweeter by Love:

> *Un Consert est charmant lors qu'il est bien d'accord,*
> *Et qu'on sçait justement suivre sa tablature;*
> *Mais il est bien plus doux, ou je me trompe fort,*
> *Quand l'Amour prend plaisir de battre la mesure.*[25]

> A Concert is charming when it is well in tune,
> And when the player knows how correctly to follow the tablature;
> But it is even sweeter, unless I'm much mistaken,
> When Love takes pleasure in beating the time.

The underlying quatrain of Nicholas Bonnart's engraving *Gentil-homme joüant de la flûte d'allemagne* (Gentleman playing the German [transverse] flute; also probably from the 1690s) reflects the fashionable use of the transverse flute by aristocratic lovers. The finely dressed gentleman boasts that he gains love skillfully by always being in style and charming with his instrument:

> *Je ne suis pas trop incommode,*
> *Je gagne un Cœur adroitement*
> *Car je suis toujours à la mode,*
> *Et charme par mon Instrument.*[26]

> I am not too unagreeable,
> I win a Heart skillfully
> Because I am always in style,
> And charm with my Instrument.

---

20. Marin Mersenne, *Harmonie universelle: Traité des instruments* (Paris, 1636); facsimile reprint, ed. François Lesure (Paris, Éditions du Centre National de la Recherche Scientifique, 1963), vol. 3, 244.

21. Anderies, "Chansons," 9.

22. Anderies, "Chansons," 9–10, 12.

23. Bowers, "Flaüste traverseinne," 29. At the Louvre.

24. Bowers, "Flaüste traverseinne," 29–30. A detail from Eustache Le Sueur's ceiling painting, *Les muses Clio, Euterpe et Thalie*, in the Hôtel Lambert in Paris, is reproduced in Bowers, "New Light," 7.

25. Bowers, "Flaüste traverseinne," 32.

26. *Ibid.*

The composer Jean-Baptiste Lully, in his ballet *Le triomphe de l'amour* (The Triumph of Love) of 1681, indicates that the highest part of a *Prelude pour l'amour* is to be played by either flute or recorder; he also designates two transverse flutes in a ritournello for an air sung by the goddess Diana.[27] The transverse flute or flutes were again called for as soft instruments in operas by Marc-Antoine Charpentier and André Campra, and in religious music by Pascal Colasse, Campra, and Charpentier,[28] including Charpentier's *Messe de minuit pour Noël* and his arrangements of noels for flutes, strings, and organ (see chap. 1). A detail of Joseph Christophe's 1711–15 painting *Baptême du dauphin, fils du Louis XIV* (Baptism of the Dauphin, Son of Louis XIV; see picture on our title page)[29] shows a children's choir accompanied by flute and recorder and directed with a rolled-up paper as baton, probably by Jean-Baptiste Lully.[30]

The d-sharp key that allowed all semitones in the octave to be played was added to the transverse flute possibly as early as the 1660s. The newly-tapered bore that permitted subtle dynamic inflections like those of human speech made the new instrument excel in touching the heart. Sebastien Brossard's *Dictionnaire de musique* (1703) describes the character of flutes, "especially the transverse ones," as *triste, languissant, &c.* (sad, languishing, etc.).[31] As late as 1740 Hubert Le Blanc, in reviewing a performance by the flutist Michel Blavet, wrote that the violin, by that time the reigning prima donna of Paris concerts, was forced to acknowledge the flute's superiority in imitating the voice:

> *Cependant, malgré tous ces avantages, le Violon rencontra dans la Flute traversière une Emule, au point où il ne s'attendoit pas, & qui rabattoit bien de la bonne opinion qu'il avoit conçue de son propre mérite, & donnée aux autres sur las nature du Son qu'il tiroit. La Flute se trouva mieux déclamer que le Violon, être plus maitresse d'enfler ou faire diminutions. Après la fin du concert on en remporta cette opinion, que la Flute joué par un Blavet, s'entend, est préférable au prémier Violon, lorsqu'il s'agit d'imiter la Voix, qui ne sauroit, comme chacun sait, faire pluseurs Tons à la fois.[32]*

However, in spite of all these advantages [such as playing double stops], the violin met a rival in the transverse flute, in a way that it hadn't expected, and which well humbled the good opinion that it had conceived of its own merit, and had given to others on the nature of the sound that it drew [with its bow]. The flute was found better to declaim than the violin, to be a greater mistress of swelling [the tone] and making diminutions [adding improvised ornamentation]. After the concert the opinion was carried away that the flute played by a Blavet is naturally preferable to the best violin when it concerns the imitation of the voice which, as everyone knows, doesn't know how to produce several tones at once.

François Raguenet (1702) commended Philbert Rebillé (called Philbert or Philibert), René Pignon Descouteaux, Pierre Philidor, and Jean and Jacques Hotteterre for the touching groans and amorous sighs they elicited from their flutes:

> *[Nous avons] les flûtes que tant d'illustres* sçavent faire gémir d'une maniere si touchante dans nos airs plaintifs, & soupirer si amoureusement dans nos airs tendres.[33]*
> **Philbert, Philidor, Descouteaux, & les Hoteterres* [Raguenet's note].

27. Bowers, "New Light," 11–12.
28. Bowers, "Flaüste traverseinne," 44–7.
29. The painting was sketched in 1711 and painted in 1715.
30. For the full painting see Pierre Marcel, *La peinture française au début du dix-huitième siècle* (Paris, 1906), 208–9. In Bowers, "New Light," 19–20. Recognition of the conductor as Lully by Patricia M. Ranum, private correspondence, January 1995.
31. In Bowers, "Flaüste traverseinne," 39.
32. Hubert Le Blanc, *Defense de la basse de viole* (Amsterdam, 1740), 49.
33. François Raguenet, *Paralele des italiens et des françois en ce qui regarde la musique et les opéra* (Brussels, 1702), facsimile reprint (Geneva: Minkoff, 1976), 18.

[We have] flutes that so many of the illustrious—Philbert, Philidor, Descouteaux, and the Hotteterres—know how to make groan in a manner so touching in our plaintive airs, and sigh so amorously in our tender ones.

Philbert and Descouteaux were the first renowned professional players of the transverse flute; they were also singers well acquainted with the vocal airs. The first quatrain of a poem by Alexandre Lainez suggests that Philbert played sweet songs by Michel Lambert (a great singer and the father-in-law of Jean-Baptiste Lully) on his flute:

> *Cherchez-vous des plaisirs, allez trouver* Philbert;
> *Sa voix, des doux chants de* Lambert,
> *Passe au bruit éclatant d'un tonnerre qui gronde:*
> *Sa Flute seule est un Concert.*[34]

If you seek pleasure, go find *Philbert*;
> His voice, from the sweet songs of *Lambert*,
Passes to the explosive noise of rumbling thunder:
> His Flute alone is a Concert.

Descouteaux's 1728 obituary reports that he was honored especially for his performance of tender little airs (*petits airs tendres*) on the flute:

> *René Pignon des Coteaux . . . est Mort à Paris le 22 Decembre, dans le 83e année de son âge, avec de grands sentimens de piété. Il avoit de grands talens pour la musique en général, avec un gout admirable pour les Chants & pour les Instrumens, sur tout pour la Flute Traversiere, dont il tiroit un son admirable, dans un temps où cet Instrument n'étoit presque point connu en France. C'est un des premiers qui l'a mis en vogue. Il ne joüoit guere que de petits airs tendres, mais avec un gout & une propreté charmante.*[35]

> René Pignon *Descouteaux . . .* died in Paris, December 22, in his 83rd year, amidst great sentiments of piety. He had great talent for music in general, with an admirable taste for singing and for playing instruments, especially the transverse flute, from which he drew an admirable sound at a time when this instrument was almost unknown in France. He was one of the first who made it popular. He played almost nothing but little tender airs, but with taste and a charming neatness.

Louis XIV had much enjoyed hearing Philbert and Descouteaux play simple airs together:

> *Il [Philbert] joüoit parfaitement de la flute Allemande, il étoit camarade de Descôteaux, célebre dans l'art de joüer de cet instrument. Louis XIV se faisoit un vrai plaisir d'entendre ces deux personnes exprimer des chants melodieux sur leurs flutes, & les faisoit souvent venir pour cela dans ses appartemens, et dans les bosquets de Versailles.*[36]

> [Philbert] played the transverse flute perfectly. He was a friend of Descouteaux, [also] celebrated in the art of playing this instrument. Louis XIV was greatly pleased to hear these two people perform pleasing melodies on their flutes, and for this had them come often into his apartments and the groves of Versailles.

---

34. Alexandre Lainez, *Poësies de Lainez* (The Hague: Aux Dépens de la Compagnie, 1753), 29. In Bowers, "Flaüste traverseinne," 35–6. For a translation of the complete poem, see Anderies, "Chansons," 15.

35. *Mercure de France* (Paris), 11 December 1728, 2896–7. In Bowers, "Flaüste traverseinne," 38, and Anderies, "Chansons," 16 (with trans.), and "Vocal Music," 1 (trans. only).

36. *Mercure de France* (Paris), 1 June 1725, 1081. In Bowers, "Flaüste traverseinne," 38, and Anderies, "Chansons," 15 (with trans.), and "Vocal Music," 1 (trans. only).

Bowers surmises that the king's pleasure in these performances may well have led to the strong and almost immediate popularity of the new instrument in France.[37]

The transverse flute soon became fashionable for aristocratic courtship in France. Antoine Watteau's painting *L'Accord parfait* (The Perfect Accord), probably from the 1710s, shows an elegantly dressed gentleman playing the transverse flute, reading his music over the shoulder of a gentle, attentive, and lovely young lady; their hair almost touches.[38] Jean Raoux's *Le Quatuor* (The Quartet) of the 1720s shows two ladies singing from a music book; one peers over the other's shoulder, a gentleman plays a transverse flute over the shoulder of the second lady, and another gentleman off to the side conducts with a rolled-up paper.[39] An engraving by Basset, *Par une tendre chansonette* (With a Tender Little Song), after the undated painting of the same name by Nicolas Lancret (1690–1743), shows a gentleman in a woodland setting playing the transverse flute for two ladies and a gentleman who pays special attention to one of the ladies.[40]

Vocal Music Played by 18th-century Flutists

Anderies points out that the publications from which flutists of the late 17th and early 18th centuries drew much of their material probably included Christophe Ballard's monthly series for singers of *Airs sérieux et à boire* (1695–1724) and the three-volume collection *Brunetes ou petits airs tendres* (1703, 1704, 1711) of the most popular 17th-century *chansons à danser, chansonettes,* and simple *airs sérieux* published by the Ballard firm during the previous century.[41] Ballard's *brunette* designation refers to the first line of the refrain of *Le beau berger Tircis,* the air on the first page of the 1703 publication. This song, like many other *brunettes,* concerns a dark-haired shepherdess:

Le beau berger Tircis,	The handsome shepherd Tircis,
Près de sa chere Annette:	Close to his dear Annette,
Sur les bords du Loir assis,	On the banks of the Loir seated,
Chantoit dessus sa musette:	Sang over his musette [kind of bagpipes]:
Ah! Petite Brunete	Ah! Little Brunette,
Ah! tu me fais mourir.[42]	Ah! you make me die.

Flutists' reliance on vocal airs was so strong that when Michel de La Barre published his first book of suites for transverse flute and bass (1702)—the first edition of pieces specifically for solo flute—he stated in the Avertissement:

Ces Piéces sont pour la plus grande partie d'un caractere si singulier & si differentes de l'idée qu'on a euë jusques icy, de celles qui conviennent à la Flute Traversiére, que j'avois resolu de ne leur faire voir le jour qu'en les executant moy-même. . . .[43]

These pieces are, for the most part, of a character so singular and so different from the idea that one has had until now of those pieces that are suited to the transverse flute, that I had resolved to have them see the light of day only by playing them myself. . . .

---

37. Bowers, "Flaüste traverseinne," 39.
38. Bowers, "New Light," 26–7, includes reproduction of the detail.
39. Bowers, "New Light," 27–8, includes reproduction of the painting.
40. Bowers, "New Light," 29–30, includes reproduction of the engraving.
41. Anderies, "Chansons," 17–18, and "Vocal Music," 1.
42. In Elissa Poole, "The Sources for Christophe Ballard's *Brunetes ou petits airs tendres* and the Tradition of Seventeenth-Century French Song," Ph.D. diss. (University of Victoria, 1985), 69. The earliest version Poole cites comes from *Airs de cour de différents autheurs,* vol. 7 (Paris: Pierre Ballard, 1626), 29.
43. Michel de La Barre, *Pièces pour la flûte traversière avec la basse continue* (Paris: Christophe Ballard, 1702), Avertissement.

The transverse flute soon had a reasonable literature of its own, yet several publications of vocal airs arranged specifically for the instrument appeared in Paris in the 1720s. Jacques Hotteterre le Romain's *Airs et brunettes* (1721) included arrangements for two or three transverse flutes without bass of several anonymous airs and *brunettes*, as well as arrangements for solo flute without bass of a few *brunettes* and a dozen *airs serieux* by Lambert, Lully, Jean-Baptist de Bousset, Henry Desmarets, and Bénigne de Bacilly. In 1725 Rippert included, besides the 16 noels that are the subject of this book, 85 airs arranged for two transverse flutes, a few with the accompaniment of an unfigured bass. Michel Pignolet de Montéclair arranged 93 *Brunetes anciènes et modernes* (c. 1721–33) for transverse flute and figured bass, inventing new melodies for old lyrics as he thought necessary. Florid *Doubles* in the elaborate vocal style of Lambert and Bacilly follow most of Hotteterre's *airs serieux*, some of his *brunettes* for solo flute, two of Rippert's *brunettes* (see ex. 2.11), and many of Montéclair's *brunettes*.

In the preface to his *Brunettes*, Montéclair touts the pedagogic value to instrumentalists of practicing little vocal airs until the basic techniques of good playing are firmly established:

> *Je crois que ceux qui aprennent a joüer des instruments ne doivent pas dans les commencements s'exercer sur des pieces difficilles que corrompent ordinairement la main, ils doivent d'abord apprendre a bien poser la main, a joüer regulierement, a former avec grace tous les sons et tous les agréments du chant et enfin a connoitre peu a peu tous les detours dont l'instrument est susceptible, . . . en peut passer ensuitte et par degrés a des musiques plus difficilles observant toujours le beau port de la main.*[44]

I believe that those who learn to play instruments must not in the beginning practice difficult pieces, which usually spoil the hand [a violinist himself, Montéclair presumably is referring to the hand on the bow and/or the fingers on the strings]. They must first learn to position the hand well, to play regularly, to form with grace all the sounds and all the melodic ornaments and finally to get to know little by little all the twists and turns of which the instrument is capable, . . . progressing then by degrees to the more difficult music, always observing the beautiful carriage of the hand.

Just because the *chansons populaires* were not technically demanding did not mean they were easy to play with the proper vocal expression. Montéclair considers "the little tender airs" by Marin Marais and François Couperin to be more difficult to perform than these masters' larger pieces:

> *Je suis persuadé que Messieurs Marais et Couperin, qui par la beauté de leurs ouvrages se sont attiré l'estime universelle, conviendront que les petits Airs tendres qu'ils ont preslé parmi leurs autres pieces, sont les plus difficilles a executer par le sentiment qu'ils demendent et qu'ils ne les affectent pas moins que leurs grandes pieces.*[45]

I am persuaded that Messieurs Marais and Couperin, who by the beauty of their works attracted universal esteem, agree that the little tender airs that they scattered among their other pieces are the most difficult to perform because of the sentiment that they demand and that affect them no less than their large pieces.

Montéclair lists "soul" as a chief ingredient needed to perform the little airs well:

---

44. Michel Pignolet de Montéclair, *Brunetes anciènes et modernes apropriées à la flûte traversière avec une basse d'accompagnement* (Paris, c. 1721–33), Preface.
45. *Ibid.*

. . . pour les petits Airs il faut, non seulement, avoir un genie naturel, un gout delicat, une disposition tendre dans la main, mais il faut encor beaucoup d'Áme pour leur donner l'expression qu'ils demendent dont tres peu de gens sont capables.[46]

. . . for the little airs, it is necessary to have not only a natural talent, a delicate taste, and a tender disposition of the hand, but one also needs a great deal of soul to give them the expression they require and of which very few people are capable.

By "a tender disposition of the hand," the violinist Montéclair refers primarily to sensitivity in the holding of the right (bow) hand and perhaps secondarily to the fingers of the left. For players of the transverse flute, this "tender disposition" must extend to the mastery of breath, tongue, and embouchure to bring forth the desired human expressions.

Besides serving as practice material for learning an instrument and performing in an unaffected style, *brunettes* were important tools for learning the art of transposition. Flutists needed to transpose in order to accompany singers in the keys best suited to their voices. Jacques Hotteterre le Romain, author of the first transverse flute method[47] and compiler of the *Airs et brunettes* for transverse flutes mentioned earlier, devotes a whole chapter of his *Art de preluder*[48] to a "Method for learning to transpose in all the clefs and on all the notes,"[49] so that flutists will learn to perform the airs in unison with both high and low voices. He uses the popular *Le beau berger Tircis* as a model, transposing it from its original key of C minor to D, E, F, G, A, and B minors.

Montéclair includes a miniature lesson in transpostion in the preface to his *Brunettes*. For each suite of *brunettes* in the anthology, he gives the transpositions that transverse flutists are most likely to need for playing with singers. To convince flutists of the rewards to be reaped from transposing, he describes a particularly moving concert he heard in which the flute played in unison with the voice:

Il faut s'exercer sur la transposition car rien n'est si touchant que d'entendre ces petits airs par une belle voix accompagneé a l'unisson par une flûte traversiere on ne doutteroit pas de ce que j'avance si, comme moy, on avoit entendu chanter Madame Perichon accompagnée par Mr. Bernier officier du Roy qui remplit si dignement, a l'opera, la place de l'illustre Mr. de la Barre qui s'en est retiré au grand regret du public, je ne sçaurois exprimer le plaisir que je sentis d'entrendre, a Boulogne, ce petit concert qui me penetra plus que n'avoit jamais fait aucune musique artistement travaillée.[50]

One must practice transposition because nothing is so touching as to hear these little airs sung by a beautiful voice accompanied in unison by a transverse flute. No one would doubt this if, like myself, they had heard Madame Perichon sing accompanied by Mr. Bernier, officer of the King who replaces so worthily at the Opera the illustrious Mr. de la Barre, who retired from it to the great regret of the public. I wouldn't know how to express the pleasure that I felt on hearing, at Boulogne, this little concert which penetrated me more than any artistically worked out music had ever done.

The unaffected, natural, yet expressive vocal lines of noels and other *brunettes* made them excellent practice material for beginning flutists. Rippert in fact dedicated his flute duet anthology on the title page to "those wishing to learn to play the transverse flute." In the present book, we broaden Rippert's purported audience to all those wishing to learn the true art of playing the little French airs.

---

46. *Ibid.*

47. Jacques Hotteterre le Romain, *Principes de la flute traversière* (Paris, 1707).

48. Jacques Hotteterre le Romain, *L'Art de préluder sur la flute traversière, sur la flute-à-bec, sur le haubois, et autres instruments de dessus* (Paris, 1719), 51–6; reprint, with resetting of type, ed. Michel Sanvoisin (Paris: Zurfluh, 1966), 60–6.

49. *Methode pour apprendre a transposer sur toutes les Clefs et sur tous les tons.*

50. *Ibid.*

PART II

❦

FLUTE DUET ANTHOLOGY

In this performance edition we present the noels in the order they appear in [Jean-Jacques?] Rippert's *Brunettes ou petits airs a II dessus*, numbering them 1 to 16. We give the complete French lyrics for all noels and name each for the first line of lyrics. Appendix 4 gives scansions and English translations for the beginning of each noel.

The Source

Two different printings of Rippert's *Brunettes ou petits airs a II dessus* are held by the Bibliothèque municipale of Lyon, France, and the Bibliothèque nationale of Paris. The Lyon holding contains only the first 14 of the 16 noels in the Paris volume; the word *FIN* follows Noel 14, and only the first 14 noel titles are listed in the Lyon contents. The title pages of the two printings differ slightly, and a fingering chart in the Paris holding replaces the *Avertissement* (Introduction; literally, Notice) and *Extrait du privilège du roi* (Royal license to publish) in the Lyon holding. Both printings are dated 1725. The engraving of the airs in the Lyon and Paris volumes is identical. Appendix 3 gives facsimiles of Rippert's title page and the 16 noels.[1]

Rippert is identified only as "M.̣ R" on the title page of both printings. According to the *Extrait du privilège* in the Lyon holding, a " S.̣ Rippert" received a license from the King of France on June 26, 1722, to publish "a collection of sonatas and other pieces for musical instruments." Whether the esteemed woodwind maker Jean-Jacques Rippert or a younger member of the family compiled and arranged the noels for transverse flutes is not known. In 1696, Jean-Jacques had been called a master maker of wind instruments and a maker of flutes, established in Paris in that profession for a long time.[2] In 1701, Joseph Sauveur named "Sieur Rippert" and "Sieur Jean Hautetaire [*sic*] le jeune" the most able makers in Paris.[3] In 1715 and 1716 Rippert built tranverse flutes for a German, von Uffenbach, who described the woodwind maker as "an old, somewhat surly grouch," but reported his flutes in demand as far east as Frankfurt.[4]

The pieces in Rippert's anthology are grouped into four suites. The second suite comprises the 16 noels. Each page is headed *Premier recüeil* (First collection [of noels]), though no other *Recüeil* of noels is included. This heading differentiates the section from the two collections of popular songs that make up the rest of the anthology: *Brunettes 1.ᵉʳ recüeil*; and *Brunettes 2.ᵉ recüeil*.

Editorial Procedures: Music

We have kept Rippert's original meter signs (2, 3, and 3/2) and notational values. We have modernized:

---

1. Taken from Betty Bang Mather's personal copy, which is identical to the Paris holding.
2. "*Jean Jacques Ripert, Maistre faiseur d'instruments à vent*" and "*Faiseur de Flutes*," in William Waterhouse, *The New Langwill Index* (London: Tony Bingham, 1993), "Rippert."
3. "*. . . les plus habiles facteurs de Paris*," idem.
4. "*. . . alten, etwas mürrischen grausen Putzer*," idem.

- the old French violin clef, which has G on the first line, to the treble clef;

- key signatures, omitting the lower octave F-sharp in the D major signature and supplying the missing B-flat in the D minor one;

- repeat signs, placing them after the second strain only where dots precede the final double bar (Rippert's original double bar between strains always includes dots on both sides, whether or not the final double bar is preceded by dots; see app. 3 facsimiles of Noels 4, 5, 8, 10, 12, and 14);

- the "white" notation of Noel 9 to "black" for easier reading (see facsimile in app. 3).

Precautionary accidentals have been added in parentheses, and editorial corrections of accidentals are shown in square brackets. Only one correction in rhythm was needed in the entire anthology (Noel 1); we have given the original notation at the bottom of its page.

To help players recognize the musical end of one line of lyrics and the start of the next, we have added breath marks to the first flute part. Usually the second flutist can breathe in the same places. In the few cases where the second flute's phrasing differs, we have placed breath marks there as well. Commas within parentheses conclude the first of two or more lines, where a breath is optional. Commas without parentheses conclude a group of lines, where a breath is necessary. In the *Doubles* (see Noels 1, 10, 13, and 14) we have placed breath marks using the first stanza as a guide.

Editorial Procedures: Lyrics

Nicolas Oudot's 1684 printing of *La Grande bible des noels tant viels que nouveaux* (Troyes and Paris) supplies our lyrics for all but Noels 2 and 14. The 1727 printing of *La Grande bible*, though closer to the date of Rippert's collection, lacks three noels (3, 8, and 16) included in the earlier printing, and the lyrics of those noels given fit Rippert's music less well. Many lines have incorrect syllable counts, resulting from unnecessary changes in verb tense (e.g., *est* in 1684 may be *étoit* in 1727), accidental omissions of words, and modernizations of the French language. Two specific instances of modernization are the one-syllable *avec* for the old, two-syllable *avecque*; and the feminine, two-syllable *grande* for the old, gender-neutral *grand*. The newer lyrics sometimes destroy the rhyme, e.g., *nouveau* for *nouvel* in Noel 13. We believe the 1684 texts better reflect how these orally transmitted tunes were sung, even in 1727; for instance, the *e* of *grande*, even where written, would have been dropped in performance.

The main concern with the 1684 source is its spelling, which is outdated by Rippert's day and does not accurately reflect pronunciation. To reach a compromise between the two sources, we have edited the 1684 lyrics to reflect Oudot's 1727 spellings, except where syllable count was affected.[5] Where variant spellings were found in both printings, we chose the more modern spelling and, for consistency, applied that to all instances of the word. We transcribed the old script *f* to the modern *s* and all consonants *u* to *v*, as well as supplying hyphens in inversions (i.e. *sont-ils venus* for *sont ils venus*). We used both *Grande bible* printings to edit Oudot's somewhat sporadic capitalization, retaining capitalized nouns that refer to religious personnages and concepts (e.g. *Fils, Mere, Esprit, Ciel, Enfer*). We have made the same changes for the lyrics by Binard (Noel 2) and

---

5. Readers familiar with modern but not older French may be helped by knowing three archaicisms still present in 1727 but not in the modern language: (1) the diphthong *-oit*, used to form the imperfect past tense, becomes *-ait* in modern French (i.e., *pourroit = pourrait, chantoit = chantait*); (2) the plural designation *-ez* for nouns ending in *-é* becomes *-és* in modern French (i.e., *qualitez = qualités*); and (3) the trema over vowels (ü, etc.) almost always disappears through modernization. The trema often shows pronunciation as a separate syllable, especially with vowels other than *u* (*venüe = ve-nu-e*).

Colletet (Noel 14). Original punctuation for all noels is retained with only slight changes for clarity.

We have corrected small typographical mistakes without comment. These include such things as agreement of subject and verb (i.e., *ils sont venu* corrected to *ils sont venus*). Where syllable counts do not fit the music, we consulted Oudot's 1727 *Grande bible*, Christophe Ballard's *Chants de noëls* (Paris, 1704; reprint 1712), Jaques Moderne's *La fleur des noelz* (Lyon, [1535]), and Pierre Sergent's *Les Grans noels* (Paris, [1537?]). In one instance we consulted a modern source, *Noël! Chantons Noël!* by Paul Arma. A footnote gives the original 1684 reading and, in parentheses, the source against which the line was modified.

The performer will still have to reconcile some lines with their syllable counts. Soft *e*'s must be dropped, and sometimes pronounced rather than elided, to make lines the correct lengths. Some examples are *grandement,* which must be *grand'ment* in Noel 10, stanza 6; *Herodes,* which must be *Herod* in Noel 12, stanza 9; and *mere et pucelle* that must *not* be elided in Noel 10, line 4. The letter *i,* when it occurs before a vowel, especially in a verb ending (i.e., *allions, étiez*), is usually pronounced with the following syllable (*al-lions, é-tiez*) but may occasionally be pronounced as a separate syllable (*al-li-ons, é-ti-ez*) to fill out the line. Diphthongs may sometimes have to be pronounced as separate vowels (especially with the past participle *oüi,* "heard") to fit the syllables to the music.

The phrase *Ainsi soit-il* (So be it) is appended at the end of some noels in Oudot's publication. We include this wherever it occurs. It may have been sung or spoken, or was perhaps a purely literary addition.

For two noels, we supply lyrics that do not match Rippert's titles; we have placed his title in brackets below ours. For Noel 14 we use the lyrics of François Colletet's 17th-century noel parody, *Quand Dieu nâquit à Noel,* from his *Noels nouveaux et cantiques spirituels* (Paris, 1665). Rippert's title, *Quand la Mer rouge apparut,* is the first line of the noel's timbre. We believe a similar situation exists for Noel 2, where we were unable to locate any lyrics using Rippert's title, *Que de gentilles pelerines.* This title may identify a secular song to which noel lyrics were set, or perhaps another parody of such a song.[6] We instead use Pierre Binard's parody on the same melody: *Quoi, ma voisine, és-tu fâchée?.* The words are taken from the 1717 printing of his *Noels ou cantiques nouveaux* (Troyes and Paris, first printing 1678).

Christophe Ballard's *Chants des noëls* is the only 18th-century source we found to include both the popular noel lyrics and music. A reproduction of the first page appears in appendix 2. Ballard includes all but Rippert's Noels 2 and 14, though for Noel 8 he uses the 2 instead of Rippert's 3 sign. His alternate version of Noel 8 shows that the word "Noel," which Oudot placed at the end of each stanza, actually follows the stanza's penultimate line.[7] Our source for fitting lyrics to the music of Noel 2 was Paul Arma's modern edition, *Noël! Chantons Noël!,* a collection drawn from a variety of sources. Our guide for Noel 14 was a modern arrangement by Joseph Canteloube.

For Noel 9, *Or nous dites Marie,* we followed Ernest Myrand's setting of the words in *Noëls anciens de la nouvelle-France.* Myrand based his transcription on the music of Simon-Joseph Pellegrin's *Chants des noels anciens* (1718). Though Pellegrin gives new words, he cites as his timbre the opening two lines of the eighth quatrain of the old noel, presumably omitting what came before (see chap. 2 for a thorough discussion).

---

6. We ask anyone who knows of such lyrics to contact us through our publisher.
7. Oudot places almost all his *Noels* at the end of the last line of each stanza. In a few instances he "slips" and puts *Noel* at the end of the penultimate line, where it belongs. Presumably the end-of-stanza placement was for appearance.

1. Où s'en vont ces gais bergers

Fl. 1

Fl. 2

[Où s'en vont ces gais ber - gers En - sem - ble côte à cô - te:

Nous al - lons voir Je - sus - Christ Né de - dans u - ne grot - te: Où est -

il le pe - tit nou - veau né, Le ver - rons - nous en - co - re?]

Double.

*original:

Ou s'en vont ces gais bergers
Ensemble côte à côte:
Nous allons voir Jesus-Christ
Né dedans une grotte:
Où est-il le petit nouveau né,
Le verrons-nous encore?[1]

Nous allons voir Jesus-Christ
Né dedans une grotte,
Pour venir avecque nous,
Margote se décrotte:

Pour venir avecque nous
Margotte se décrotte,
Aussi fait la belle Alix
Qui a troussé sa cotte:

Aussi fait la belle Alix
Qui a troussé sa cotte,
De peur du mauvais chemin
Craignant qu'on ne la crotte:

De peur du mauvais chemin
Craignant qu'on ne la crotte,
Janneton n'y veut venir
Elle fait de la sotte:

Janneton n'y veut venir
Elle fait de la sotte,
Disant qu'elle a mal au pied
Et veut que l'on la porte:

Disant qu'elle a mal au pied
Et veut que l'on la porte,
Robin en ayant pitié
A apprêté sa hotte:

Robin en ayant pitié
A apprêté sa hotte,
Janneton n'y veut entrer
Voyant bien qu'on se mocque:

Janneton n'y veut entrer
Voyant bien qu'on se mocque,
Aime mieux aller à pied
Que de courir la poste:

Aime mieux aller à pied
Que de courir la poste,
Tant ont fait les bons bergers
Qu'ils ont vû cette grotte:

Tant ont fait les bons bergers
Qu'ils ont vû cette grotte,
En l'étable où n'y avoit
Ni fenêtre ni porte:

En l'étable où n'y avoit
Ni fenêtre ni porte,
Ils sont tous entrés dedans
D'une ame très-devote:

Ils sont tous entrés dedans
D'une ame très-devote,
Là ils ont vû le Sauveur
Dessus la chenevotte:

Là ils ont vû le Sauveur
Dessus la chenevotte,
Marie est auprés pleurant,
Joseph la reconforte:

Marie est auprés pleurant
Joseph la reconforte,
L'âne et le bœuf aspirant,
Chacun d'eux le rechauffe:

L'âne et le bœuf aspirant
Chacun d'eux le rechauffe,
Contre le vent froid cuisant
Lequel souffle de côte:

Contre le vent froid cuisant
Lequel souffle de côte,
Les pasteurs s'agenoüillant
Un chacun d'eux l'adore:

Les pasteurs s'agenoüillant
Un chacun d'eux l'adore,
Puis s'en vont riant, dansant
La courante et la volte:

Puis s'en vont riant, dansant
La courante et la volte,
Prions le doux Jesus-Christ
Qu'enfin il nous conforte:

Prions le doux Jesus-Christ
Qu'enfin il nous conforte,
Et nôtre ame au dernier jour
Dans les Cieux il transporte:

---

1. The refrain *Où est-il le petit nouveau né, Le verrons-nous encore?* is sung after each stanza. To conserve space, we have omitted it in the remaining stanzas.

2. Quoi, ma voisine, és-tu fâchée?

[Rippert: *Que de gentilles pelerines*]

[*L'Humble:* Quoi, ma voi - sine, és - tu fâ - ché - e: Dis - moi pour - quoi?
Veux - tu ve - nir voir l'a - cou - ché - e: A - vec - que moi?

C'est u - ne Da - me fort dis - cre - te, Ce m'a - t-on dit,

Qui nous a pro - duit le Pro - phe - te, Sou - vent pré - dit.]

Des bergeres en dialogue, l'une humble et l'autre mondaine.

L'Humble:
Quoi, ma voisine, és-tu fâchée:
Dis-moi pourquoi?
Veux-tu venir voir l'acouchée:
Avecque moi?
C'est une Dame fort discrete,
Ce m'a-t-on dit,
Qui nous a produit le Prophete,
Souvent prédit.

La Mondaine:
Je le veux, allons ma commere,
C'est mon desir,
Nous verrons l'Enfant et la Mere
Tout à loisir:
Aurons-nous pas de la dragée,
Et du gateau?
La salle est-elle bien rangée,
Y fait-il beau?

L'Humble:
Ha! ma bergere tu te trompes,
Fort lourdement,
Elle ne demande pas les pompes,
Ni l'ornement;
Dedans une chetive étable,
Se veut ranger,
Ou n'y a ni buffet ni table,
Pour y manger.

La Mondaine:
Au moin est-elle bien coiffée,
De fin réseaux,
Et sa couche est-elle étoffée,
De beaux rideaux,
Son ciel n'est-il pas de brodure,
Tout campané,
N'a-t-il pas pour bordure,
L'or bazané?

L'Humble:
Elle a pour sa plus belle couche
Dans ce lieu,
Le tronçon d'une vieille souche,
Tout au milieu:
Le mur lui sert d'une custode,
Et pour son ciel
Il est fait à la pauvre mode,
De chaume vieil.

La Mondaine:
Encore faut-il que l'accouchée
Ait un berceau,
Pour bercer quand elle est couchée,
L'Enfant nouveau?
N'a-t'elle pas garde et servante
Pour la servir?
N'est-elle pas assez puissante,
D'y subvenir?

L'Humble:
L'Enfant a pour berceau la crêche,
Pour sommellier,
Et une botte d'herbe seiche,
Pour oreiller:
Elle a pour toute compagnie
Son cher Baron
Elle a un bœuf sa menie,
Et un ânon.

La Mondaine:
Tu me dégoûtes, voisine,
D'aller plus loin,
Pour voir une femme gesine,
Dessus du foin:
Pour moi, qui ne suis que bergere,
Suis beaucoup mieux,
Que non pas cette menagere,
Sous un toit vieux.[1]

L'Humble:
Ne parle plus ainsi commere,
Mais par honneur,
Crois-moi que c'est la chaste Mere
Du vrai Sauveur,
Qui veut ainsi humblement naître,
Nous sauvant tous,
Montrant que bien qu'il soit le Maître,
Et humble et doux.

Exempte nous, très chere Dame,
De tout orgüeil,
Quand du corps partira nôtre ame,
Fais-lui accüeil,
La presentant (grande Princesse)
A ton cher Fils
Pour participer la liesse
Du Paradis. Amen. Noel Noel Noel.

---

1. Sous toit vieux (after Paul Arma, *Noël! Chantons Noël!*)

67

3. Laissez paître vos bêtes

[Lais - sez paî - tre vos bê - tes, Pas - tou - reaux, par monts et par vaux Lais -

sez paî - tre vos bê - tes Et ve - nez chan - ter Nau. Nau.

J'ay oüi chan - ter le ros - si - gnol Qui chan - toit un chant si nou - veau, Si haut, si

beau, si ré - son - neau Il m'y rom - poit la tê - te Tant il prê - choit et

ca - que - toit, A - donc pris ma hou - let - te Pour al - ler voir Nau - let.]

68

Laissez paître vos bêtes,
Pastoureaux, par monts et par vaux
Laissez paître vos bêtes
Et venez chanter Nau.

J'ay oüi chanter le rossignol
Qui chantoit un chant si nouveau,
Si haut, si beau, si résonneau[1]
Il m'y rompoit la tête
Tant il prêchoit et caquetoit,
Adonc pris ma houlette
Pour aller voir Naulet.

Je m'enquis au berger Naulet,
As-tu oüi le rossignolet,
Tant joliet, qui gringotoit,
Là haut sur une épine?
Oüi dit-il, je l'ay oüi,
J'en ay pris ma bussine,
Et m'en suis réjoüi.

Nous dîmes tous une chanson
Les autres y sont venus au son,
Or sus dançons, prens Alison
Je prendray Guillemette,
Et Margot prendra gros Guillot:
Qui prendra Perronnelle?
Ce sera Talebot.

Ne parlons plus, nous tardons trop,
Allons y tôt, courons le trot,
Viens tôt Margot, attens Guillot:
J'ay rompu ma courette,
Il faut recoutrer mon sabot:
Or tiens cette éguillette,
Elle te servira trop.

Comment Guillot, ne viens-tu pas?
Oüi, j'y vais tout le doux pas,
Tu n'entend pas du tout mon cas
J'ay aux talons les mules,
Parquoi je ne puis plus trotter,
Prise m'ont les froidures
En allant étraquer.

Marche devant, pauvre mullart
Et t'appuye sur ton billart,
Et toi Coquart, vieil loriquart
Tu deusses avoir grand honte
De rechiner ainsi les dents,
Et deusse en tenir conte,
Au moins devant les gens.

Nous courûmes de telle roideur
Pour voir nôtre doux Redempteur
Et Créateur, et Formateur,
Il avoit (Dieu le sçache)
Des drapeaux assez grand besoin,
Il gisoit en la crêche
Sur un petit de foin.

Sa Mere avecque lui étoit,
Un vieillard qui les éclairoit,
Pas à l'Enfant ne résembloit,
Il n'étoit pas son pere
Je l'aperçû trop bien et beau
Résembloit à la Mere,
Encore est-il plus beau.

Or nous avions un gros paquet
De vivres pour faire un banquet
Mais le muguet de Jean Huguet
Et une grand levriere
Mirent le pot à découvert,
Ce fut par la bergere[2]
Qui laissa l'huis ouvert.

Pas ne laissâmes de gaudir
Je lui donnay une brebis
Au petit Fils une mauvis,
Lui donna Perronnelle:
Margot si lui donna du lait,
Toute pleine une écuelle
Couverte d'un volet.

Or prions tous le Roi des Rois
Qui nous donne à tous bon Noel
Et bonne paix de nos méfaits
Ne veüille avoir memoire
De nos pechez mais pardonner
A ceux de Purgatoire
Nos pechez effacer. Ainsi soit-il.

---

1. Oudot 1684 reads *Si bon, si beau...*, but all other versions we have seen use *haut,* which creates an internal rhyme with *beau* and *résonneau.*

2. Mais ce fut par la bergere (Sergent)

4. Vous qui desirez sans fin

[Vous qui de - si - rez sans fin, Oü - ir chan - ter
Que nô - tre Dieu est en - clin, A é - cou - ter

Nô - tre pri - ere et com - plain - te Tous les jours,

Quand nous in - vo - quons sans fein - te Son se - cours.]

Vous qui desirez sans fin,
Oüir chanter
Que nôtre Dieu est enclin,
A écouter
Nôtre priere et complainte
Tous les jours,
Quand nous invoquons sans feinte
Son secours.

Et comme il est tout prêt
De pardonner,
Non pas d'un severe arrêt
Nous condamner,
Nôtre mal et nôtre peine
Relâchant,
Oyez de la Magdelaine
Le beau chant.

Magdelaine se levoit,
Etant au jour,
Et bravement se paroit
D'un bel atour,
Quand Marthe, moins curieuse
Des habits,
Là vint aborder, joyeuse
Par ces dits:

Dieu soit nôtre Protecteur
Ma chere sœur,
Si vous voulez en ce temps
Pour passe-temps,
Voir quelque chose de rare
Et de beau,
Oyez ce qui se prepare
De nouveau.

Un Prophete est arrivé,
Bien approuvé,
Dit Jesus de Nazareth,
Homme discret,
Qui devoit faire à l'instance
(Ce dit-on)
D'une divine éloquence
Le sermon.

C'est l'homme le plus parfait
Et en effet,
Le plus beau, le plus sçavant
Le mieux disant,
Que jamais vîtes en face
Pour certain,
Son port avec telle grace
N'est humain.

Magdelon, oyant ceci
Prend ses habits,
De beau velours cramoisi
Les plus jolis,
De sa blonde chevelure
Tout en rond,
Faisant mille tortillures
Sur son front.

Ainsi parée d'habits
Beaux et polis,
S'en va nôtre Magdelon
A ce sermon,
Qui ne faut à prendre place
Près sa sœur,
Droit vis-à-vis de la face
Du Sauveur.

Aussi-tôt qu'elle entendit
Cet Orateur,
Boüillonner elle sentit
Le sang au cœur,
Puis une couleur vermeille,
A loisir,
Cette face blanche et belle
Vint saisir.

Bref sa voix tant excita
De saints desirs,
Que dès l'heure, elle quitta
Tous ses habits,
Voüant de saintement vivre
Desormais,
Et cette doctrine ensuivre
Pour jamais.

Quand fut fini le sermon
On se départ,
Jesus s'en va chez Simon,
Et autre part,
Magdelaine sort honteuse
Soûpirant,
Sa piasse somptueuse
Va laissant.

Elle prend donc tout subit
Un simple habit,
Ses cheveux ayant éparts
De toutes parts,
En sa main une boëte[1]
D'un onguent,
Va de loin le saint Prophete
Poursuivant.

Arrivant chez le lepreux
Où il dînoit,
De son onguent precieux
Qu'elle tenoit,
Oignit le chef et la tête
Du Sauveur,
Parfumant toute sa tête
De l'odeur.

Puis s'abaissant à ses pieds
Les essuya,
De ses cheveux déliés
Qu'elle déploya,
Les lavant de l'abondance
De ses pleurs,
Jettoit cris de repentance
Et clameurs.

Quand Simon eut ceci vû
S'en étonnoit,
Jesus l'ayant aperçû,
L'en reprenoit,
Puis dit à la Magdelaine
T'es commis,
Et pechez sans nulle peine
Sont remis.

Or prions ce bon Sauveur
De bouche et cœur,
Qu'ainsi qu'il a fait pardon
A Magdelon,
Ainsi que chantions la gloire
De ces faits,
Il ôte de sa memoire
Nos forfaits. Ainsi soit-il.

---

1. Et en sa main une boëte (Oudot 1727)

5. Chantons je vous prie

Fl. 1

[Chan-tons je vous pri - e   No-el hau - te-ment,   De Ma - rie pu -
D'u - ne voix jo - li - e,   En so - lem - ni - sant,

Fl. 2

cel - le   La con-cep - ti - on,   Sans o - ri - gi - nel - le   Ma - cu - la - ti - on.]

Chantons je vous prie
Noel hautement,
D'une voix jolie,
En solemnisant,
De Marie pucelle
La conception,
Sans originelle
Maculation.

Cette jeune Fille
Native elle étoit,
De la noble ville
Dite Nazareth,
De vertu remplie
De corps gratieux,[1]
C'est la plus jolie
Qui soit sous les Cieux.

Elle alloit au temple
Pour Dieu supplier,
Le conseil s'assemble
Pour les marier,
La Fille tant belle
N'y veut consentir,
Car Vierge et pucelle
Veut vivre et mourir.

L'Ange lui commande
Qu'on fasse assembler,
Gens en une bande
Tous à marier,
Et duquel la verge
Tantôt fleurira,
A la noble Vierge
Vrai mari sera.

Tantôt abondance
De gentils galands,
La Vierge plaisante
Vont tous souhaitant,
A la noble Fille
Chacun s'attendoit,
Mais le plus habile,
Sa peine il perdoit.

Joseph prit sa verge
Pour s'y en venir,
Combien qu'à la Vierge
N'eût mis son desir,
Car toute sa vie
N'eut intention,
Vouloir, ni envie
De conjonction.

Quant ils furent au temple
Trestous assemblés,
Etant tous ensemble
En troupe ordonné,
La verge plaisante
De Joseph fleurit,
Et à même instance
Porta fleur et fruit.

En grand reverence,
Joseph on retint,
Qui par sa main blanche
Cette Vierge print,
Puis après le prêtre
Recteur de la loi,
Leur a fait promettre
A tous deux la foi.

Baissant les oreilles,
Ces gentils galands,
Tant que c'est merveilles
S'en vont murmurans,
Disant, c'est dommage
Que ce pere gris
Ait en mariage
La Vierge de prix.

La nuit ensuivante
Autour de minuit,
La Vierge plaisante
En son livre lit,
Que le Roi celeste
Prendroit nation,
D'une pucelette
Sans corruption.

Tandis que Marie
Ainsi contemploit,
Et du tout ravie
Envers Dieu étoit,
Gabriël l'Archange
Vint subtilement,
Entra dans sa chambre
Tout visiblement.

D'une voix doucette
Gracieusement:
Dit à la Filette
En la salüant,
Dieu vous gard Marie
Pleine de beauté;
Vous êtes l'amie
De la Déïté.

Dieu fait un mystere
En vous merveilleux,
C'est que serez Mere
Du Roi glorieux,
Vôtre pucelage
Et virginité,
Par divin ouvrage
Vous sera gardé.

A cette parole
La Vierge consent
Le Fils de Dieu volle
En elle descend
Tantôt fut enceinte
Du Prince des Rois
Sans mal ni sans crainte
Le porta neuf mois.

La noble besogne
Joseph pas n'entend
A peur qu'il n'en gronde
S'en va murmurant,[2]
Mais l'Ange celeste
Lui dit en dormant,
Qu'il ne s'en déhaitte,
Car Dieu est l'Enfant.

Joseph et Marie
Tous deux Vierges sont,
Qui par compagnie
En Bethléem vont,
Là est accouchée
En pauvre déduit
La Vierge sacrée
Autour de minuit.

Elle fut consolée
Des anges des Cieux
Elle fut visitée
Des pasteurs joyeux
Elle fut reverée[3]
Des trois nobles rois,
Elle fut rejettée[4]
Des riches bourgeois.

Or prions Marie
Et Jesus son Fils,
Qu'après cette vie
Nous donne Paradis,
Et nôtre voyage
Etant achevé,
Ayons pour partage
Le Ciel azuré. Ainsi soit-il.

---

1. De ce corps glorieux (Oudot 1727)

---

2. Sans va murmurant (Oudot 1727)
3. Elle fut visitée (Oudot 1727)
4. Elle fut reverée (Oudot 1727)

6. Tous les bourgeois de Châtre

Fl. 1

Fl. 2

[Tous les bour - geois de Châ - tre Et ceux de Mont - l'he - ry,
Me - nez tou - te grand joy - e Cet - te jour - née i - ci,

Que nâ - quit Je - sus - Christ De la Vier - ge Ma - ri - e, Où le bœuf

et l'â - non don don, En - tre les - quels cou - cha la la, En u - ne ber - ge - ri - e.]

Tous les bourgeois de Châtre
Et ceux de Mont-l'hery,[1]
Menez toute grand joye
Cette journée ici,
Que nâquit Jesus-Christ
De la Vierge Marie,
Où le bœuf et l'ânon don don,
Entre lesquels coucha la la,
En une bergerie.

Les anges ont chanté
Une belle chanson,
Aux pasteurs et bergers
De cette region,
Qui gardoient leurs moutons
Paissant la bergerie,
Disant que le mignon don don,
Etoit né près de là la la,
Jesus le fruit de vie.

Laisserent leurs troupeaux
Paissant parmi les champs;
Prirent leurs chalumeaux,
Vinrent dançant chantant,
Et droit à Saint Clement
Menant joyeuse vie,
Pour visiter l'Enfant si grand,
Lui donnant des joyaux si beaux
Jesus les remercie.

Puis ceux de Saint Germain,
Tous en procession,
Partirent bien matin
Pour trouver l'enfançon,
Puis oüirent le son
Et la douce harmonie,
Que saisoient ces pasteurs joyeux,
Lesquels n'étoient pas las, la la,
De mener bonne vie.

Les farceurs de Bruieres
N'étoient pas endormis
Sortirent des tanieres
Quasi tous étourdis,
Les rueurs de Boissy
Passerent la chaussée,
Cuidant avoir oüi le bruit
Et aussi les débats la la,
D'une très-grosse armée.

Puis eussiez vû venir
Tous ceux de Saint Yon,
Et ceux de Bretigni,
Apportant du poisson,
Les barbeaux et gardons
Anguilles et carpettes,
Etoient à bon marché, croyez
A cette journée-là, la la,
Et aussi les perchettes.

Lors ceux de Saint Clement
Firent bien leur devoir
De faire asseoir les gens
Qui venoient voir le Roi,
Joseph les remercie
Et aussi fait la Mere,
Les eussiez vû dancer, chanter
Et mener grand soulas la la,
En faisant tous grand chere.

Bas des Hymnes a joüé
De son beau tabourin,
Car il étoit loüé
A ceux de Saint Germain,
La grand bouteille au vin
Ne fut pas oubliée,
Ratissant du rebec joüet
Car avec eux alla la la,
Cette digne journée.

Lors un nommé Corbon
Faisoit de bon broüet
A la soupe à l'oignon
Cependant qu'on dançoit,
Lapins et perdreaux
Alloüettes rôties,
Canards et cormorans frians
Gilet Badaut porta la la,
A Joseph et Marie.

Avecque eux étoit
Un du païs d'Amont
Qui du luth resonnoit
De très-belles chansons,
De Châtre les mignons
Menoient grand rusterie,
Les Eschevins menoient, portoient
Trompettes et clairons don don
En belle compagnie.

Messire Jean Guyot
Le vicaire d'Egly
Apporta plein un pot
Du vin de son logis,
Messieurs les écoliers
Toute icelle nuitée,
Se sont pris à chanter, danser,[2]
Ut re mi fa sol la la la,
A gorge déployée.

Puis il en vint trois autres
Lesquels n'étoient pas las,
Qui dedans une chause
Lui firent hypocras,
Et Jesus étoit là
Qui les regardoit faire,
Le morveux le passa, coula,
En dressant en tâta la la,
Joseph en voulut boire.

Ce sont pris à dancer
De si bonne façon,
Et puis en ont fait boire
Au gentil ratisson,
Lequel le trouva bon
Comme il nous fit accroire,
Puis demanda pardon très-bon,
Et si remercia la la,
Jesus aussi sa Mere.

Nous prions tous Marie,
Et Jesus son cher Fils,
Qu'ils nous donnent leur gloire
Là sus en Paradis,
Après qu'aurons vêcu
En ce mortel repaire,
Qu'il nous veüille garder d'aller
Tous en Enfer la bas la la,
En tourment et misere.

---

1. Les bourgeoises de Chastre /
Et de Mont-le hery (Ballard).
Though Oudot's 1684 lyrics fit the
music, almost all arrangements we
have seen (including Rippert's and
Charpentier's) begin *Tous les
bourgeois de Châtre / Et ceux de....*
The subject *bourgeoises* is feminine
rather than masculine. The change
to the masculine is reflected in
Oudot 1727, which reads *Les
bourgeois de Chartres* (though the
omission of Tous causes the line to
lack one syllable).

2. Se sont pris à chanter de
het (Oudot 1727)

7. Noel pour l'amour de Marie

Fl. 1 / Fl. 2

[No - el pour l'a - mour de Ma - ri - e Nous chan - te -

rons joy - eu - se - ment, Quand elle por - ta le fruit de

vi - e Ce fut pour nô - tre sau - ve - ment.]

76

Noel pour l'amour de Marie
Nous chanterons joyeusement,
Quand elle porta le fruit de vie
Ce fut pour nôtre sauvement.

Joseph et Marie s'en allerent
Un soir bien tard en Bethléem,
Ceux qui tenoient hôtellerie
Ne les prisoient pas grandement.

S'en allerent parmi la ville
Et d'huis en huis logis querant,
A l'heure la Vierge Marie
Etoit bien près d'avoir Enfant.

S'en allerent chez un riche homme
Logis demander humblement,
Et on leur repondit en somme:
Avez-vous chevaux largement?

Nous avons un bœuf et un âne,
Voyez-les ci presentement:
Vous ne semblez que trüandaille
Vous ne logerez point céans.

Ils s'en allerent chez un autre
Logis demander pour argent,
Et on leur respondit en outre,
Vous ne logerez point céans.

Joseph si regarda un homme
Qui l'appella méchant païsant,
Où veux-tu mener cette femme
Qui n'a pas plus haut de quinze ans?

Joseph va regarder Marie
Qui avoit le cœur très-dolent,
En lui disant, ma douce amie
Ne logerons-nous autrement.

J'ay vû là une vieille étable,
Logeons-nous y pour le present,
Alors la Vierge aimable
Etoit bien près d'avoir Enfant.

A minuit en cette nuitée,
La douce Vierge eut Enfant,
Sa robe n'étoit point fourrée
Pour l'enveloper chaudement.

Elle le mit en une créche
Sur un peu de foin seulement,
Une pierre dessous sa tête
Pour reposer le Roi puissant.

Très-cheres gens, ne vous déplaise
Si vous vivez bien pauvrement,
Si fortune vous est contraire
Prenez le tout patiemment.

En souvenance de la Vierge
Qui prit son logis pauvrement,
En une étable découverte
Qui n'étoit point fermée devant.

Or prions la Vierge Marie
Que son Fils veüille supplier
Qu'il nous doit mener telle vie
Qu'en Paradis puissions entrer.

Si une fois y pouvons être
Jamais ne nous faudroit plus rien,
Ainsi fut logé nôtre Maître,
Le doux Jesus, en Bethléem.

8. A minuit fut fait un réveil

A minuit fut fait un réveil[1] *bis*
Jamais n'en fut oüi un pareil *bis*
Au pays de Judée, Noel,
Au pays de Judée.

Les pasteurs étant endormis, *bis*
Veilloient leurs moutons et brebis *bis*
Le long d'une verd prée, Noel,[2]
Le long d'une verd prée.

Ebahis furent grandement *bis*
Quand en moins d'un petit moment *bis*
Oüirent comme une armée, Noel,
Oüirent comme une armée.

C'étoient plusieurs anges des Cieux *bis*
Qui faisoient un bruit merveilleux *bis*
Tant devant que derriere, Noel,
Tant devant que derriere.

Entr'autres étoit Gabriël, *bis*
Messager du Roi eternel *bis*
Parlant de telle maniere, Noel,
Parlant de telle maniere.

Ne craignez point, mes bons amis, *bis*
Pour vous annoncer suis transmis *bis*
La paix universelle, Noel,
La paix universelle.

Nôtre Sauveur sur terre est né *bis*
Comme il a été ordonné, *bis*
Par le conseil celeste, Noel,
Par le conseil celeste.

---

1. A minuict fait un réveil (Oudot 1727)
2. Le long d'un verd pré (Ballard)

En Bethléem le trouverez, *bis*
En une étable où le verrez, *bis*
Couché entre deux bêtes, Noel,
Couché entre deux bêtes.

Les pasteurs, ayant entendu *bis*
Ce mandement, tant attendu, *bis*
S'assemblent de vitesse, Noel,
S'assemblent de vitesse.

Gomabut Rifflard et Alory *bis*
Robin, Marion, et Alix, *bis*
Se trouverent à l'adresse, Noel,
Se trouverent à l'adresse.

Comme aussi fit Colin Jaquet *bis*
Et Margot avec son caquet, *bis*
Menant la Perronnelle, Noel,
Menant la Perronnelle.

Puis s'y trouva étant bien las *bis*
Le bon berger Gillet Thomas, *bis*
Et Alison Grimbelle, Noel,
Et Alison Grimbelle.

Etant assemblés sont partis *bis*
Laissant leurs moutons et brebis, *bis*
Paissant sur l'herbelette, Noel,
Paissant sur l'herbelette.³

Vers Bethléem ont pris chemin *bis*
Chacun tendant à cette fin *bis*
De voir ce Roi celeste, Noel,
De voir ce Roi celeste.

En allant, Rifflard devisoit *bis*
De quoi c'est qu'on l'étrenneroit, *bis*
Mais Gombaut vint à dire, Noel,
Mais Gombaut vint à dire:

Quand à moi mon present est prêt, *bis*
C'est un aigneau qui sans arrêt, *bis*
Pris en ma bergerie, Noel,
Pris en ma bergerie.

Alors répondit Alory, *bis*
Je lui donneray ma brebis, *bis*
Laquelle est si jolie, Noel,
Laquelle est si jolie.

Robin a dit à Marion, *bis*
A l'eternel Roi de Sion, *bis*
Que donnerons-nous, ma mie, Noel,
Que donnerons-nous, ma mie?

Marion lui a répondu, *bis*
J'ay un bel œuf tout frais pondu, *bis*
Pour mettre en sa boüillie, Noel,
Pour mettre en sa boüillie.

A l'instant répondit Robin, *bis*
Je lui donneray le gratin; *bis*
En seras-tu marrie, Noel,
En seras-tu marrie?

Comment, ce dit Colin Jaquet *bis*
Faut-il avoir tant de caquet, *bis*
Que ne courons-nous vîte, Noel,
Que ne courons-nous vîte?

Il me tarde que je n'y suis, *bis*
Dit Margot, je voudrois voir l'huis, *bis*
Dieu que tant il m'ennuie, Noel,
Dieu que tant il m'ennuie.

Nos presens sont en ce paquet *bis*
Avec ceux de Colin Jaquet, *bis*
Et de sa grand amie, Noel,
Et de sa grand amie.

Ce dit Catin, le mien est beau, *bis*
C'est une tarte et un gâteau, *bis*
Suis-je pas bien garnie, Noel,
Suis-je pas bien garnie.

Lors répondit Gillet Thomas, *bis*
Et ma foi le mien n'y est pas, *bis*
Dont j'en ay fâcherie, Noel,
Dont j'en ay fâcherie.

Il est serré bien dignement *bis*
Et envelopé richement, *bis*
Ce n'est point mocquerie, Noel,
Ce n'est point mocquerie.

Si vous voulez sçavoir le don, *bis*
C'est une flute et un bedon, *bis*
Pour réjoüir Marie, Noel,
Pour réjoüir Marie.

En babillant se sont trouvés, *bis*
Près Bethléem où sont trouvés, *bis*
Pour voir ce fruit de vie, Noel,
Pour voir ce fruit de vie.

Layant trouvé l'ont adoré *bis*
Et de leurs presens decoré *bis*
Ne face non marrie, Noel,
Ne face non marrie.

Ayant fait, ont quitté le lieu *bis*
Se recommandant au bon Dieu, *bis*
Et aussi à Marie, Noel,
Et aussi à Marie.

Or prions le devotement *bis*
Que nôtre ame au définement *bis*
Soit és saints Cieux ravie, Noel,
Soit és saints Cieux ravie.

---

3. Pasturans sur l'herbelette. Oudot (1684) gives
two different lines for this identical couplet; we have
retained the line with the correct syllable count.

9. Or nous dites Marie *

*original in white notation. See facsimile (appendix example 3.9).

†original:
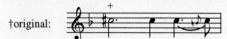

Or nous dites Marie
Où étiez-vous alors,
Quand Gabriël l'Archange
Vous fit un tel record?

J'étois en Galilée
Plaisante region,
En ma chambre enfermée,
En contemplation.

Or nous dites Marie
Cet Ange Gabriël,
Ne dit-il autre chose
En ce salut nouvel?

Tu concevras Marie,
Dit-il sans fiction,
Le Fils de Dieu t'assie,
Et sans corruption.

Or nous dites Marie
En presence de tous,
A ces douces paroles
Que respondîtes-vous?

Comment se pourroit faire
Qu'en telle nation,
Le Fils de Dieu mon Pere,
Prenne incarnation.

Or nous dites Marie
Vous sembla-t-il nouvel,
D'oüir telles paroles
De l'Ange Gabriël?

Oüi, car de ma vie
Je n'eus intention,
D'avoir d'homme lignée,
Ni copulation.

Or nous dites Marie,
Que vous dit Gabriël,
Quand vous vit ébahie
De ce salut nouvel.

Marie ne te soucie
C'est l'obombration,
Du saint Esprit ma mie
Et l'operation.

Or nous dites Marie,
Creustes-vous fermement,
Ce que l'Ange vint dire
Sans nul empêchement?

Oüi, disant à l'Ange
Sans autre question,
Soit faite et accomplie
Ta nonciation.

Or nous dites Marie
Les neuf mois accomplis,
Nâquit le fruit de vie
Comme l'Ange avoit dit?

Oüi, sans nulle peine
Et sans oppression,
Nâquit de tout le monde
La vrai Redemption.

Or nous dites Marie
Du lieu imperial,
Fut-ce en chambre parée,
Où en palais royal?

En une pauvre étable
Ouverte à l'environ,
Où n'avoit feu ni flamme,
Ni latte, ni chevron.

Or nous dites Marie
Qui vous vint visiter,
Les bourgeois de la ville
Vous ont-ils rien donné?

Oncques homme ni femme
N'en eut compassion,
Non plus que d'un esclave
D'étrange region.

Or nous dites Marie
Les laboureurs des champs,
Vous ont-ils visitée,
Et aussi les marchands?

Je fus abandonnée
De cette nation,
Et d'eux en la nuitée
N'eus consolation.

Or nous dites Marie
Les pauvres pastoureaux,
Qui gardoient és montagnes,
Leurs brebis et agneaux?

Ceux-là m'ont visitée,
Par grande affection,
Sçachez que fort m'agrée
Leur visitation.

Or nous dites Marie
Les princes et les rois,
Vôtre Enfant débonnaire,
Le sont-ils venus voir?

Trois rois de haut parage,
D'étrange region,
Lui vinrent faire hommage
Et grande oblation.

Or nous dites Marie
Que devint cet Enfant,
Tandis qu'il fut en vie
Fut-il homme sçavant?

Homme de sainte vie
Et grand devotion
Etoit, je vous affie
Sans nulle abusion.

Or nous dites Marie
Puisque l'Enfant fut né,
Tant comme il fut en vie
Fut-il du monde aimé?

Oüi, n'en doutez mie,
Fors de la nation,
Des faux juifs pleins d'envie,
Et de deception.

Or nous dites Marie
Les faux juifs malheureux,
Lui portoient-ils envie
Tant qu'il fut avec eux?

Telle envie lui porterent
Et sans occasion,
Que souffrir ils lui firent
Cruelle passion.

Or nous dites Marie
Sans plus en enquerir,
Ces faux juifs pleins d'envie
Le firent-ils mourir?

Oüi, de mort amere
Par grand detraction,
En la Croix le cloüerent
Et entre deux larrons.

Or nous dites Marie
En étiez-vous bien loin,
Fûtes-vous la presente,
En vîtes-vous la fin?

Oüi las! éplorée
Par grande affection,
Dont souvent chûë pâmée,
Et non pas sans raison.

Nous vous prions Marie
De cœur très-humblement,
Que nous soyez amie[1]
Vers vôtre cher Enfant:
Afin qu'és jours funestes[2]
Que tous jugés seront
Puissions être pourvûs,
Là sus avec les bons. Ainsi soit-il.

_____

1. Que nous soyons amie (Oudot 1727)
2. Afin qu'és jours venus (Oudot 1727)

10. Joseph est bien marié

Fl. 1

[Jo - seph est bien ma - ri - é, Jo - seph est bien ma - ri -
A la Fil - le de Jes - sé, A la Fil - le de Jes -

Fl. 2

é, C'é - toit cho - se bien nou - vel - le, D'ê - tre me - re et pu -
sé,

cel - le, Dieu y a bien o - pe - ré, Jo - seph est bien ma - ri - é.]

Double.

82

Joseph est bien marié, *bis*
A la Fille de Jessé, *bis*
C'étoit chose bien nouvelle,
D'être mere et pucelle,
Dieu y a bien operé,
Joseph est bien marié.

Et quand ce vint au premier *bis*
Que Dieu nous voulut sauver *bis*
Il fit en terre descendre
Son seul Fils Jesus pour prendre
En Marie humanité,
Joseph est bien marié.

Quand Joseph eut aperçû *bis*
Que sa femme avoit conçû *bis*
Il ne s'en contenta mie,
Fâché fut contre Marie,
Et s'en voulut en aller
Joseph est bien marié.

Mais l'Ange si lui a dit, *bis*
Joseph, n'en aye dépit, *bis*
Ta sainte femme Marie
Est grosse du fruit de vie:
Elle a conçû sans peché,
Joseph est bien marié.

Change donc ton pensement, *bis*
Et approche hardiment, *bis*
Car par sa toute-puissance
Tu és durant son enfance
A le servir dedié,
Joseph est bien marié.

A Noel en droit minuit, *bis*
Elle enfanta Jesus-Christ, *bis*
Sans peine et sans tourment,
Joseph se soucie grandement
Du cas qui est arrivé,
Joseph est bien marié.

Les anges y sont venus, *bis*
Voir le Redempteur Jesus, *bis*
De très-grande compagnie,
Puis à haute voix jolie
Gloria ils ont chanté
Joseph est bien marié.

Les pasteurs ont entendu, *bis*
Que le Sauveur est venu, *bis*
Ont laissé leurs brebiettes,
En chantant de leurs musettes,
Disant que tout est sauvé,
Joseph est bien marié.

Les trois rois pareillement *bis*
Ont apporté leurs presens, *bis*
Or, encens, aussi du myrrhe,
Ont donné au Fils Marie,[1]
De lui sortoit grand clarté
Joseph est bien marié.

Or prions devotement *bis*
De bon cœur très-humblement, *bis*
Que paix, joye et bonne vie
Impetre Dame Marie,
A nôtre necessité,
Joseph est bien marié.

---

1. Ont donné au fils de Marie (Sergent). There are one too many syllables in this line, due to the modernization of "fils Marie" to "fils de Marie."

11. Une jeune pucelle

Fl. 1 / Fl. 2

[U - ne jeu - ne pu - cel - le de no - ble cœur,
Pri - ant en sa cham - bret - te son Cré - a -

teur, L'An - ge du Ciel de - scen - dit sur la ter - re Lui

con - ta le my - ste - re De nô - tre Sal - va - teur.]

Une jeune pucelle de noble cœur,
Priant en sa chambrette son Créateur,
L'Ange du Ciel descendit sur la terre
Lui conta le mystere
De nôtre Salvateur.

La pucelle ébahie de cette voix,
Elle se prit à dire pour cette fois,
Comment pourra s'accomplir telle affaire
Car jamais n'eus affaire
De nul homme qui soit.

Ne te soucie Marie aucunement,[1]
Celui qui seigneurie au firmament,
Son saint Esprit te fera apparoître
Dont tu pourras connoître
Tôt cet enfantement.

Sans douleur ni sans peine et sans tourment,
Neuf mois seras enceinte de cet Enfant,
Et quand viendra à le poser sur terre
Jesus faut qu'on l'appelle,
Roi sur tout triomphant.

Lors fut tant consolée de ses beaux dits,
Qu'elle s'estimoit être en Paradis,
Se soûmettant du tout à lui complaire:
Disant voici l'ancelle,
Du Sauveur Jesus-Christ.

Mon ame magnifie, Dieu mon Sauveur
Mon esprit glorifie son Créateur:
Car il a eu égard à son ancelle,
Que terre universelle
Lui soit gloire et honneur.

---

1. This line was probably sung by dropping the mute
-*e* on *soucie* and pronouncing the one on *Marie*.

12. Voici le jour solemnel

Fl. 1

Fl. 2

[Voi - ci le jour so - lem - nel De No - el, Qu'il

faut que cha - cun s'ap - prê - te Pour en can - tiques et chan -

sons A hauts sons, Ce - le - brer la sain - te fê - te.]

86

Voici le jour solemnel
De Noel,
Qu'il faut que chacun s'apprête
Pour en cantiques et chansons
A hauts sons,
Celebrer la sainte fête.

Le Fils de Dieu étant né
Destiné
Pour sauver l'humain lignage;
Trois rois sont partis de loin,
Avec soin,
Pour lui venir faire hommage.

Ils partirent d'Orient
En riant,
Aveque leur compagnie,
Le sont venus adorer,
Reverer,
Demenant joyeuse vie.

L'étoille les a conduits
Jours et nuits,
Jusqu'au païs de Judée,
Où étant tous parvenus
Et venus;
La ville ils ont demandée.

L'astre qui les conduisoit
Et guidoit
S'évanoüit de leur vûë,
Dont ils furent bien troublez,
Etonnez
De l'avoir si tôt perduë.

Donc en pensant être au lieu
Là où Dieu
Devoit prendre sa naissance
Ils se sont partout equis
Et requis,
Leurs en donner connoissance.

Dites-nous, mes bons seigneurs
Les docteurs,
N'est-ce pas en cette ville,
Où est né des juifs le grand Roi
Sans arroy,
D'une pucelle gentille?

Long-temps a qu'avons connu
Et prévû,
Son étoile en nôtre terre,
Qui nous a toûjours guidez
Et menez,
Jusqu'en ce lieu sans enquerre.

Herodes ayant oüi ce bruit
Il s'enfuit,
Droit jusqu'en la synagogue
Des juifs, en leur demandant
Où l'Enfant,
Etoit né, selon leur code.

Lors les docteurs lui ont dit
Et prédit
Que selon la Prophetie,
Bethléem étoit le lieu
Où ce Dieu
Viendroit nous rendre la vie.

Le tyran, oyant ceci,
Dit ainsi,
Aux rois par ruse et cautelle,
Allez et le lieu trouvez
Si pouvez,
Puis m'en rapportez nouvelle.

Etant revenus vers moi,
Sans émoi,
Avec vous j'irai sans feinte,
Adorer ce Roi nouveau
Au berceau,
Sans nulle force ou contrainte.

Mais le traître malheureux
Envieux,
Avoit bien autre pensée,
Comme il le montra exprès
Tôt après,
Aux enfans de la contrée.

Les trois rois, étant partis
Et sortis
De Jerusalem la belle,
S'éjoüirent ensemblement
Grandement,
Apercevant leur étoille.

Elle ne les laissa plus
Au surplus,
Qu'ils ne fussent en l'étable
Dans Bethléem où l'Enfant
Triomphant
Tenoit son pauvre habitacle.

Nonobstant ne laissant pas
De ce pas,
Lui faire la reverence,
L'adorant tous d'un accord
Sans discord,
Comme portoit leur puissance.

Ils ont offert leurs presens
De l'encens,
Myrrhe, or, et bonne monnoye
Puis par l'Ange détournez,
Retournez,
S'en vont par une autre voye.

13. A la venuë de Noel

[A la ve - nu - ë de No - el Cha - cun se doit bien ré - joü - ir, Car c'est un tes - ta - ment nou - vel Que tout le mon - de doit te - nir.]

Double.

*original:

†first four measures of *Double* repeated in original

A la venuë de Noel
Chacun se doit bien réjouir,
Car c'est un testament nouvel
Que tout le monde doit tenir.

Quand par son orgüeil Lucifer
Dedans l'abime trebucha
Nous allions trestous en Enfer,
Mais le Fils Dieu nous racheta.[1]

Dedans la Vierge s'en ombra,
Et dans son corps voulut gesir,
La nuit de Noel enfanta
Sans peine et sans douleur souffrir.

Incontinent que Dieu fut né
L'Ange l'alla dire aux pasteurs,
Lesquels se prirent à chanter
Un chant qui étoit gracieux.

Après un bien petit de temps
Trois rois le vinrent adorer:
Lui apportant myrrhe et encens,
Et or, qui est fort à loüer.

A Dieu le vinrent presenter,
Et quand ce vint au retourner,
Trois jours et trois nuits sans cesser
Herodes les fit pourchasser.

Une étoille les conduisoit
Qui venoit devers Orient,
Qui à l'un et l'autre montroit
Le chemin droit en Bethléem.

Nous devons bien certainement
La voye et le chemin tenir,
Car elle nous montre vrayement
Où nôtre Dame doit gesir.

Là virent le doux Jesus-Christ,
Et la Vierge qui le porta:
Celui qui tout le monde fit,
Et les pecheurs ressuscita.

Bien apparut qu'il nous aima
Quand à la Croix pour nous fut mis
Dieu le Pere qui tout créa,
Nous donne à la fin Paradis.

Prions-le tous qu'au dernier jour
Quand tout le monde doit finir,
Que nous ne puissions nulz de nous[2]
Nulle peine d'Enfer souffrir.

Amen. Noel, Noel, Noel,
Je ne me pourrois plus tenir,
Que je ne chante ce Noel,
Quand je voy mon Sauveur venir.

---

1. Mais le Fils de Dieu nous racheta (Sergent/
Moderne). Oudot's line has one too many syllables
because of the modernization of the archaic genitive
construction "le Fils Dieu" to "le Fils de Dieu." It is
possible that Oudot's line could be sung as is by singing
"racheta" as two syllables: "rach(e)ta," but we believe reinstating the archaism is a better alternative.

---

2. Que nous ne puissions aucun de nous (Sergent).
This line has too many syllables, due to the modernization of "nulz" to "aucun."

14. Quand Dieu nâquit à Noel

[Rippert: *Quand la Mer rouge apparut*]

Fl. 1

[Quand Dieu nâ - quit à No - el De - dans la Ju - dé -
On vit ce jour so - lem - nel La joye in - non - dé -

Fl. 2

e,
e; Il n'é - toit pe - tit ni grand Qui n'ap - por - tât___ son pre -

sent, Et no, no, no, no, Et ne frit, frit, frit; Et no, no, et ne

frit, Et n'of - frit sans ces - se Tou - te sa ri - ches - se.]

Double.

Quand Dieu nâquit à Noel	Ce bon Pere putatif	Quoi qu'il n'en eût pas besoin,
Dedans la Judée,	De Jesus mon Maître,	Jesus nôtre Maître;
On vit ce jour solemnel	Que le pasteur plus chétif	Il en prit avecque soin
La joye innondée;	Desiroit connoître;	Pour faire connoître
Il n'étoit petit ni grand	D'un air obligeant et doux	Qu'il avoit les qualitez
Qui n'apportât son present,	Recevoit les dons de tous,	Par ces dons representez,
Et no, no, no, no,	Sans cé, cé, cé, cé,	D'un vrai, vrai, vrai, vrai,
Et ne frit, frit, frit;	Sans ré, ré, ré, ré,	D'un Roi, Roi, Roi, Roi,
Et no, no, et ne frit,	Sans cé, cé, sans ré, ré,	D'un vrai, vrai, d'un Roi, Roi,
Et n'offrit sans cesse	Sans ceremonie	D'un vrai Roi de gloire,
Toute sa richesse.	Pour le fruit de vie.	En qui l'on doit croire.
L'un apportoit un anneau	Il ne fut pas jusqu'aux rois	Plaise à ce divin Enfant
Avec un grand zele,	Du rivage more,	Nous faire la grace,
L'autre un peu de lait nouveau	Qui joints au nombre de trois;	Dans son sejour triomphant
Dedans une écuelle;	Ne vinssent encore:	D'avoir une place:
Tel, sous ses pauvres habits,	Ces bons princes d'Orient	Si nous y sommes jamais,
Cachoit un peu de pain bis	Offrirent en le priant	Nous goûterons une paix,
Pour la, la, la, la,	L'en, l'en, l'en, l'en, l'en,	De lon, lon, lon, lon,
Pour la sain, sain, sain,	Cens, cens, cens, cens, cens,	De gue, gue, gue, gue,
Pour la, la, pour la sain,	L'en, l'en, l'en, cens, cens, cens,	De l'on, l'on, de gue, gue,
Pour la sainte Vierge,	L'encens, et la myrrhe,	De longue durée
Et Joseph concierge.	Et l'or qu'on admire.	Dans cet Empirée.

15. Grace soit renduë

Fl. 1

[Gra - ce soit ren - du - ë A Dieu de là sus, Qui nâ - quit de

De la bien - ve - nu - ë De son Fils Je - sus,

Fl. 2

Vier - ge Sans cor - rup - ti - on, Pour nô - tre dé - char - ge Souf - frit pas - si -

on, Al - le - lu - ia, Al - le - lu - ia, Ky - ri - e, Chri - ste, Ky - ri - e e - le - i - son.]

92

Grace soit renduë
A Dieu de là sus,
De la bienvenuë
De son Fils Jesus,
Qui nâquit de Vierge
Sans corruption,
Pour nôtre décharge
Souffrit passion,
Alleluia, Alleluia,
Kyrie, Christe,
Kyrie eleison.

Adam nôtre pere
Nous mit en danger
De la pomme chere
Qu'il voulut manger,
Il nous mit en voye[1]
De damnation,
Mais Dieu nous envoye
A salvation,
Alleluia, Alleluia,
Kyrie, Christe,
Kyrie eleison.

Dieu donne bonne vie[2]
A nôtre bon Roi,
Le garde d'envie
Et mortel defroy,
Lui donne victoire
De ses ennemis,
A la fin la gloire
De son Paradis,
Alleluia, Alleluia,
Kyrie, Christe,
Kyrie eleison.

Lui étant fidéles
Nous conservera,
Et toutes querelles
Il appaisera,
Rendant la justice
Aux petits et grands
Punissant le vice
Nous rendant contens,
Alleluia, Alleluia,
Kyrie, Christe,
Kyrie eleison.

Nous ferons prieres
Generalement,
Pour pere et pour mere,
Sœurs, freres et parens,
Pour toutes les ames
Qui sont en prison,
Que Dieu, par sa grace
Nous fasse pardon,
Alleluia, Alleluia,
Kyrie, Christe,
Kyrie eleison.

Grace aussi faut rendre
Au Sauveur Jesus,
Qui de sa viande
Nous à tous repûs,
Pain, vin, et fruitage
Et bon feu aussi,
Pour lui rendre hommage
Crions lui mercy,
Alleluia, Alleluia,
Kyrie, Christe,
Kyrie eleison.

Voisins et voisines
Bienvenus soyez,
Pour chacun chopine
Ne vous enfuyez,
Car suivant les traces
De nos peres vieux,
Faut boire après graces
Pour être joyeux,
Alleluia, Alleluia,
Kyrie, Christe,
Kyrie eleison.

Avant que sortir
De cette maison,
Vous veux advertir
Qu'avecque raison,[3]
Chacun verse à boire
Encore une fois,
Puis que l'on s'envoise
Et à Dieu soyez,
Alleluia, Alleluia,
Kyrie, Christe,
Kyrie eleison.

---

1. Il nous mit en joye (Oudot 1727)
2. Probably sung by dropping the -*e* on *donne* and
pronouncing the one on *bonne* (Oudot 1727; Oudot
1684 gives the old version: *Dieu doint bonne vie*)

3. Qu'avec raison. This is our correction based on
other instances in Oudot's texts.

16. Je me suis levé par un matinet

Fl. 1

[Je me suis le - vé___ par un ma - ti - net,

Fl. 2

Que l'au - be pre - noit son blanc man - te - let, Chan - tons No -

let, No - let, No - let, Chan - tons No - let en - co - re.]

94

Je me suis levé par un matinet,
Que l'aube prenoit son blanc mantelet,
Chantons Nolet, Nolet, Nolet,
Chantons Nolet encore.

Que l'aube prenoit son blanc mantelet,
J'ay pris ma jacquette et mon haut bonnet,
Chantons Nolet, Nolet, Nolet,
Chantons Nolet encore.

J'ay pris ma jacquette et mon haut bonnet,
Et mon court manteau de gris violet,
Chantons Nolet, Nolet, Nolet,
Chantons Nolet encore.

Et mon court manteau de gris violet
Je m'en suis allé chercher Colinet,
Chantons Nolet, Nolet, Nolet,
Chantons Nolet encore.

Je m'en suis allé chercher Colinet,
Qui se promenoit en son jardinet,
Chantons Nolet, Nolet, Nolet,
Chantons Nolet encore.

Qui se promenoit en son jardinet
Que faites-vous là gentil garçonnet?
Chantons Nolet, Nolet, Nolet,
Chantons Nolet encore.

Que faites-vous là gentil garçonnet?
J'écoute dit-il le rossignolet,
Chantons Nolet, Nolet, Nolet,
Chantons Nolet encore.

J'écoute dit-il le rossignolet,
Jamais je n'ay oüi chant si doucelet,
Chantons Nolet, Nolet, Nolet,
Chantons Nolet encore.

Jamais je n'ay oüi chant si doucelet,
Ce n'est rossignol ni autre oiselet,
Chantons Nolet, Nolet, Nolet,
Chantons Nolet encore.

Ce n'est rossignol ni autre oiselet,
Mais du saint Empire un saint angelet,
Chantons Nolet, Nolet, Nolet,
Chantons Nolet encore.

Mais du saint Empire un saint angelet,
Qui dit en son chant un cas nouvelet,
Chantons Nolet, Nolet, Nolet,
Chantons Nolet encore.

Qui dit en son chant un cas nouvelet?
C'est qu'en Bethléem nous est né Nolet,
Chantons Nolet, Nolet, Nolet,
Chantons Nolet encore.

C'est qu'en Bethléem nous est né Nolet,
Et que nous allions voir l'Enfantelet,
Chantons Nolet, Nolet, Nolet,
Chantons Nolet encore.

Et que nous allions voir l'Enfantelet,
J'ay pris mon tambour et mon flageolet,
Chantons Nolet, Nolet, Nolet,
Chantons Nolet encore.

J'ay pris mon tambour et mon flageolet,
Colin sa viole et son archelet,
Chantons Nolet, Nolet, Nolet,
Chantons Nolet encore.

Colin sa viole et son archelet,
Les autres bergers vinrent au ballet,
Chantons Nolet, Nolet, Nolet,
Chantons Nolet encore.

Les autres bergers vinrent au ballet,
Dieu veüille sçavoir comme tout alloit,
Chantons Nolet, Nolet, Nolet,
Chantons Nolet encore.

Dieu veüille sçavoir comme tout alloit
Le ballet fini, partîmes d'illec,
Chantons Nolet, Nolet, Nolet,
Chantons Nolet encore.

Le ballet fini, partîmes d'illec,
Et allâmes voir le petit doüillet,
Chantons Nolet, Nolet, Nolet,
Chantons Nolet encore.

Et allâmes voir le petit doüillet,
Que sa Mere couche en un drapelet,
Chantons Nolet, Nolet, Nolet,
Chantons Nolet encore.

Que sa Mere couche en un drapelet,
Chacun presenta son don joliet,
Chantons Nolet, Nolet, Nolet,
Chantons Nolet encore.

Chacun presenta son don joliet,
L'un de la farine, et de l'autre du lait,
Chantons Nolet, Nolet, Nolet,
Chantons Nolet encore.

L'un de la farine et l'autre du lait,
Puis recommençant un autre couplet,
Chantons Nolet, Nolet, Nolet,
Chantons Nolet encore.

Puis recommençant un autre couplet,
Nous prenons congé du saint agnelet,
Chantons Nolet, Nolet, Nolet,
Chantons Nolet encore.

Nous prenons congé du saint agnelet,
Chacun s'en retourne à son troupelet,
Chantons Nolet, Nolet, Nolet,
Chantons Nolet encore. Ainsi soit-il.

95

APPENDIX 1
Facsimile of Three Noels from
La fleur des noelz [Moderne, 1535]

Courtesy of the Biblioteca Colombina, Seville, Spain

APPENDIX EXAMPLE 1.1. *A la venuë de Noel* (Noel 13).

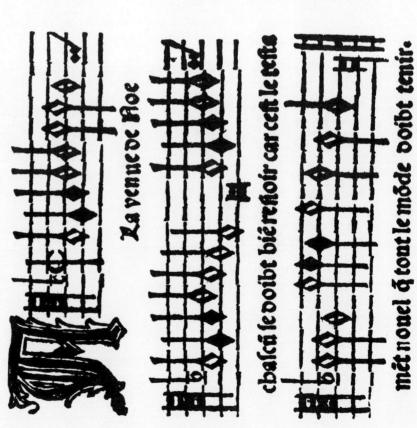

APPENDIX EXAMPLE 1.2. On "Trahison, Dieu te mauldie"
(*Noel pour l'amour de Marie*: Noel 7).

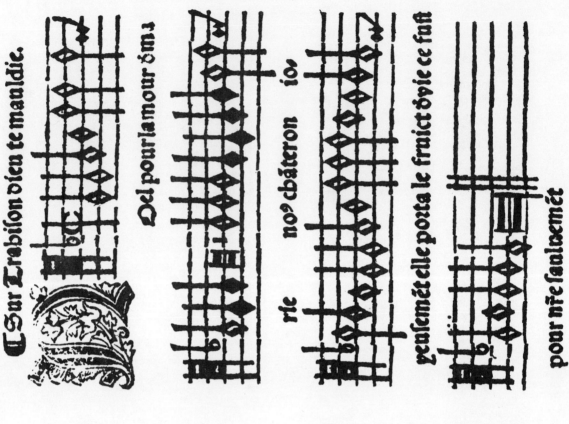

APPENDIX EXAMPLE 1.3. New Noel. *Laissez paitre vos bêtes* (Noel 3).

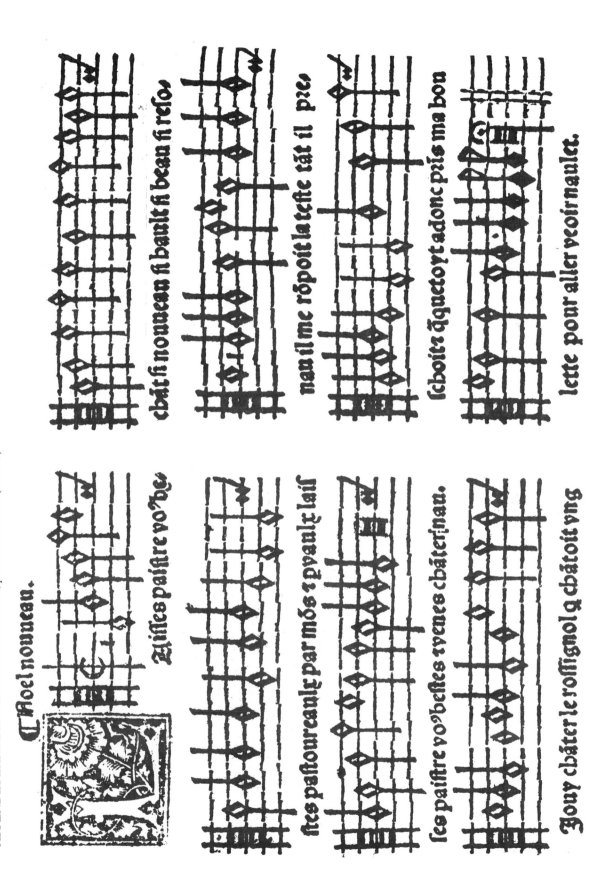

APPENDIX 2

Facsimile of First Page
from *Chants des noëls de la Grande bible*
(Ballard, 1704/12)

Courtesy of the Österreichische Nationalbibliothek, Vienna, Austria

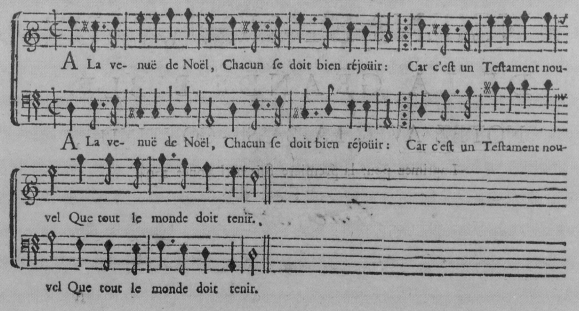

APPENDIX 3

Facsimile of Noels
from *Brunettes ou petits airs a II dessus* (Rippert, 1725)

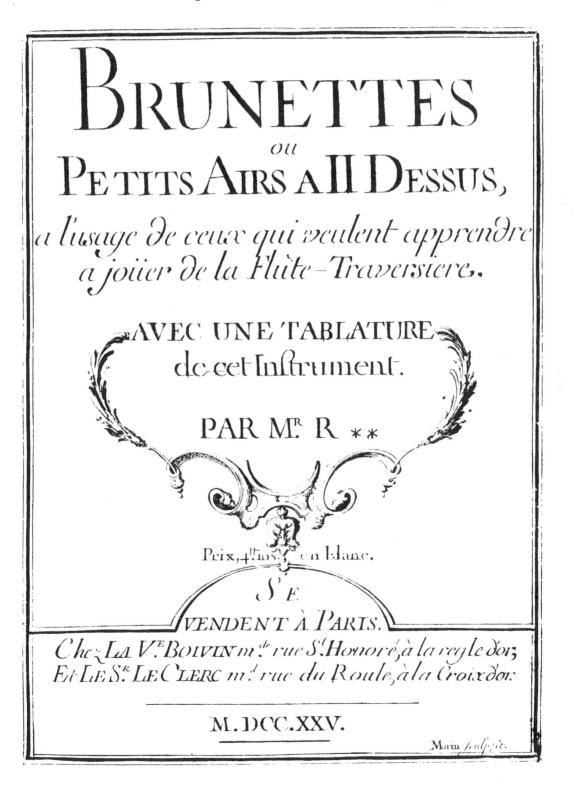

24

Premier Recüeil..

NOELS.

Ou s'en vont ces gays Bergers

Double.

Premier Recueil.

Que de gentilles pelerines

Laissez paître vos bestes

26

Premier Recueil.

Premier Recueil.

Tendrement.

Noël pour l'amour de Marie

Tendrement;

A minuit fut fait un reveil

Tres lentement.

Or nous dites Marie

28

Premier Recueil.

Premier Recueil.

Voicy le jour solemnel

A la venue de Noel

Double.

30

Premier Recueil.

Quand la Mer rouge apparut

Double.

Premier Recueil.

Graces soient rendues

Je me suis levée par un matinet

Fin du I.er Recueil.

APPENDIX 4

Scansions and English Translations of First Stanzas

A group of one to six syllables forms a unit. The unit may be an exclamation or verbal command. It may be a subject, verb, or object, though a pronoun subject or object groups with the verb. It may be a prepositional or relative phrase, or a second group begun a conjunction. It may be an adjective or adverb that immediately follows its noun or verb (one that precedes is grouped with its noun or verb). A real or implied punctuation mark suggests the end of a unit. A feminine ending may detach itself from its word to begin the next unit; if followed by a vowel, the soft *e* is elided. Our translations are as word-by-word as possible to help those unfamiliar with the French language follow the French scansion.

Noel 1

Où s'en vont / ces gais bergers
Ensem-/ ble cô-/ t(e) à côte:
Nous allons voir / Jesus-Christ
Né / dedans une grotte:
Où est-il / le pe-tit nou-veau né,
Le verrons-nous / encore?

Where are they going, / these happy shepherds,
Together / side / by side?
We are going to see / Jesus Christ,
Born / inside a grotto.
Where is He, / the little newborn?
Will we see Him / yet?

Noel 2

Quoi, / ma voisine, / és-tu fâchée:
Dis-moi / pourquoi?
Veux-tu venir / voir / l'acouchée:
Avecque moi?
C'est une Dame / fort discrete,
Ce m'a-t-on dit,
Qui nous a produit / le Prophete,
Souvent prédit.

What, / my neighbor lass, / are you angry?
Tell me / why?
Do you wish to come / to see / the new mother
With me?
She is a lady / very discreet,
So I was told,
Who for us has produced / the prophet
Often foretold.

Noel 3

Laissez paître / vos bêtes,
Pastoureaux, / par monts / et par vaux
Laissez paître / vos bêtes
Et venez chanter Nau.

Let graze / your flocks,
Shepherds, / by mountains / and by valleys,
Let graze / your flocks,
And come sing Noel.

J'ay oüi chanter / le rossignol
Qui chantoit / un chant / si nouveau,
Si bon, / si beau, / si résonneau
Il m'y rompoit / la tête
Tant il prêchoit / et caquetoit,
Adonc pris / ma houlette
Pour aller voir / Naulet.

I heard singing / the nightingale,
Who sang / a song / so new,
So good, / so beautiful, / so resonant;
It ruptured / my head [gave me a headache],
So much it preached / and chattered;
Then I took / my staff
To go see / Naulet.

Noel 4

Vous qui desirez / sans fin,
Oüir chanter
Que nôtre Dieu / est enclin,
A écouter
Nôtre prie-/ r(e) et complainte
Tous les jours,
Quand nous invoquons / sans feinte
Son secours.

You who desire / without end
To hear singing,
That our God / is inclined
To listen
To our prayer / and lament
Every day,
When we invoke / without pretence
His help.

Noel 5

Chantons / je vous prie
Noel / hautement,
D'une voix / jolie,
En solemnisant,
De Marie / pucelle
La conception,
Sans originelle
Maculation.

Let us sing, / I pray you,
Noel / strongly
With a voice / beautiful,
In solemn celebration
Of Mary / the Maiden,
The conception
Without original
Sin.

Noel 6

Tous les bourgeois / de Châtre
Et ceux / de Mont-l'héry,
Menez / toute grand joye
Cette journée / ici,
Que nâquit / Jesus-Christ
De la Vierge Marie,
Où le bœuf / et l'ânon / don don,
Entre lesquels / coucha / la la
En une bergerie.

All the burghers / of Châtre
And those / of Mont-l'héry,
Feel / all great joy
This day / here,
Because was born / Jesus Christ
Of the Virgin Mary,
Where the ox / and the ass / don don,
Between them / he slept / la la,
In a manger.

Noel 7

Noel / pour l'amour / de Marie
Nous chanterons / joyeusement,
Quand elle porta / le fruit / de vie
Ce fut / pour nôtre sauvement.

Noel / for the love / of Mary
We will sing / joyously:
When she carried / the fruit /of life,
It was / for our salvation.

Noel 8

A minuit / fut fait / un réveil *bis*
Jamais / n'en fut oüi / un pareil *bis*
Au pays / de Judée, / Noel,
Au pays / de Judée.

At midnight / was made / an awakening; *bis*
Never / was heard / one like it *bis*
In the land / of Judea, / Noel,
In the land / of Judea.

Noel 9

Or nous dites / Marie
Où étiez-vous / alors,
Quand Gabriël / l'Archange
Vous fit / un tel record?

Now tell us, / Mary,
Where were you / then,
When Gabriel / the archangel
Made you / such an announcement?

J'étois / en Galilée
Plaisante region,
En ma cham-/br(e) enfermée,
En contemplation.

I was / in Galilee,
Pleasant region,
In my chamber / enclosed,
In contemplation.

Noel 10

Joseph / est bien marié, *bis*
A la Fil-/ le de Jessé; *bis*
C'étoit chose / bien nouvelle,
D'être mere / et pucelle,
Dieu / y a bien operé,
Joseph est bien marié.

Joseph / is indeed married *bis*
To the daughter / of Jesse; *bis*
It was a thing / very new
To be [both] mother / and maid;
God / acted very well.
Joseph / is indeed married.

Noel 11

Une jeune pucelle / de noble cœur,
Priant en sa chambrette / son Créateur,
L'An-/ ge du Ciel / descendit / sur la terre
Lui conta / le mystere
De nôtre Salvateur.

A young maiden / of noble heart,
Praying in her small chamber / to her Creator:
The Angel / of Heaven / descended / onto the earth;
He told her / the mystery
Of our Savior.

Noel 12

Voici le jour / solemnel
De Noel,
Qu'il faut / que chacun s'apprête
Pour / en canti-/ qu(e)s et chansons
A hauts sons,
Celebrer / la sainte fête.

This is the day / solemn
Of Christmas,
So it is necessary / that each prepare
To, / with cantiques / and chansons,
At full voice,
Celebrate / the holy feast.

Noel 13

A la venu-/ ë de Noel
Chacun se doit / bien réjoüir,
Car c'est un testament / nouvel
Que tout le mon-/ de doit tenir.

At the coming / of Christmas,
Each must / indeed rejoice,
Because it is a testament / new
That all the world / must keep.

Noel 14

Quand Dieu nâquit / à Noel
Dedans la Judée,
On vit ce jour / solemnel
La joye / innondée;
Il n'étoit petit / ni grand
Qui n'apportâ*t* / son present,
Et no, no, / no, / no,
Et ne frit, / frit, / frit;
Et no, no, / et ne frit,
Et n'offrit / sans cesse
Toute sa richesse.

When God was born / on Christmas
In Judea,
One saw this day / of solemnity
Joy / overwhelming;
There was no one small / or big
Who did not bring / his present,
And did not, / not, / not,
Offer not, / not, /not;
And did not, / offer not,
And did not offer / without end
All his riches.

Noel 15

Gra-/ ce soit renduë
A Dieu / de là sus,
De la bienvenuë
De son Fils / Jesus,
Qui nâquit / de Vierge
Sans corruption,
Pour nôtre décharge
Souffrit / passion,
Alleluia, / Alleluia,
Kyrie, / Christe,
Kyrie / eleison.

Thanks be rendered
To God / on high
For the welcoming
Of His son / Jesus,
Who was born / of a virgin
Without corruption;
For our release,
He suffered / agony.
Alleluia / Alleluia,
Lord, / Christ,
Lord / have mercy.

Noel 16

Je me suis levé / par un matinet,
Que l'au- / be prenoit / son blanc mantelet,
Chantons Nolet, / Nolet, / Nolet,
Chantons Nolet / encore.

I woke up / one new morning
When the dawn / put on / her white cloaklet.
Let us sing / Noel, / Noel, / Noel,
Let us sing Noel / again.

BIBLIOGRAPHY

15TH THROUGH 18TH CENTURIES

Das Andernacher Gesangbuch. Cologne, 1608. Facsimile reprint, Düsseldorf: Schwann, 1970.

Aneau, Barthélémy. *Chant natal, contenant sept noelz, ung chant pastoural et ung chant royal, avec ung mystere de la nativité, par personnages.* Lyon: Sebastian Gryphius, 1539.

Arbeau, Thoinot [Jean Tabourot]. *Orchesographie, metode, et teorie en forme de discours et tablature pour apprendre a dancer, battre le Tambour en toute sorte et diversité de batteries, jouër du fifre et arigot, tirer des armes et escrimer, avec autres honnestes exercices fort convenables à la jeunesse.* Lengres: Jehan des Preyz, 1588. 2nd ed., 1589; 3rd ed., 1596. [2nd ed. titled *Orchesographie, et traicte en forme de dialogue, par lequel toutes personnes peuvent facilement apprendre et practiquer l'honneste exercice des dances.*] Translation of second edition by Mary Stewart Evans with corrections, new introduction, and notes by Julia Sutton, and Labanotation by Mireille Backer and Julia Sutton, New York: Dover, 1967. Facsimile reprint of 3rd edition, Geneva: Minkoff, 1972.

Arena, Antonius de [Antoine]. *Ad suos compagnons studiantes qui sunt de persona friantes bassas dansas de novo bragarditer.* 1519 or later. [32 eds. from 1529–1710.]

Arnoullet, Olivier, publ. *Noelz nouveaulx nouvellement faitz et composez.* Lyon, c. 1517–67.

Bacilly, Bénigne de. *Remarques curieuses sur l'art de bien chanter.* Paris, 1668. Facsimile reprint, Geneva: Minkoff, 1974.

Ballard, Christophe, publ. *Chants des noëls, anciens et nouveaux de la grande bible.* Paris, 1712 [1st printing, 1704]. Österreichischer Nationalbibliothek.

Ballard, Jean-Baptiste-Christophe, publ. *La clef des chansonniers: ou recueil des vaudevilles depuis cent ans et plus, notez, et recueillis pour la première fois.* Paris, 1717.

Ballard, Pierre, publ. *Airs de cour de différents autheurs.* Vol. 7. Paris, 1626.

Binard, Pierre. *Noëls ou cantiques nouveaux sur la nativité de nostre seigneur Jésus-Christ.* Paris, 1717. [1st ed., 1678.]

Bonfons, Jehan, publ. *Les grans noelz nouvellement imprimés à Paris pour Jean Bonfons* (c. 1543–66). Paris, Bibliothèque nationale, Imp. Rés. Pet. Ye 2648³.

Browne, William. *Allemando di Guillermo Bruno alias Janetton.* Christ Church Music MS 89; Berlin Staatsbibliothek MS 40316. In *Spanish Netherlands Keyboard Music*, edited by Richard Veudome and Colin Good, vol. 2, 26–7. Oxford: John Brennan, 1993.

Charpentier, Marc-Antoine. "Energie des modes." *Règles de composition.* Paris, Bibliothèque nationale, MS n.a. fr. 6355, f. 13–13v. Facsimile reprint and annotated translation in Lillian M. Ruff, "Marc-Antoine Charpentier's *Règles de composition*," *Consort* 24 (1968): 233–70.

————. *Messe de minuit pour Noël.* Paris, Bibliothèque nationale, MS Rés., Vm¹ 259; tome 25, f. 62–77. Edited by H. Wiley Hitchcock. St Louis, Mo.: Concordia Publishing House, 1962.

————. *Noëls sur les instruments.* Paris, Bibliothèque nationale, MS Rés., Vm¹ 259; tome 5.

Colletet, François. *Noels nouveaux et cantiques spirituels, nouvellement composez et mis en lumiere, sur les plus beaux airs de cour et chants de ce temps.* Paris: Antoine Rafflé, 1665. Paris, Bibliothèque de l'Arsenal, B. L. 8017. Reprint, 1669; Bibliothèque de Tours, 2473.

Coplande, Robert. *Here Followeth the Manner of Dancing Bace Dances after the Use of France and Other Places translated out of French in English by Robert Coplande*, appendix to *The Introductory to Write and to Pronounce French*, by Alexander Barclay. London, 1521. Reprint, Flansham, Sussex: Pear Tree Press, 1937.

Cotgrave, Randle. *A Dictionarie of the French and English Tongues.* London, 1611.

Dandrieu, Jean-François. *Noëls, O filii, chansons de Saint Jacques, et carillons. Le tout extrèment varié et mis pour l'orgue et pour le clavecin* (Paris, [?1721–33]). Edited by Gaston Litaize and Jean Bonfils as *Noëls*, L'Organiste Liturgique nos. 19–20, Paris: Editions musicales de la Schola cantorum et de la Procure générale de musique, 1955.

Daquin, Louis-Claude. *Nouveau livre de noëls pour l'orgue et le clavecin dont la plûpart peuvent s'exécuter sur les violons, flûtes, hautbois, etc., Oeuvre II.* Paris, c. 1740. Edited by Norbert

Dufourcq, Félix Raugel, and Jean de Valois as *Nouveau livre de noëls*, Orgue et liturgie nos. 27–8, Paris: Editions musicales de la Schola cantorum et de la Procure générale de musique, n.d.

Furetière, Antoine. *Dictionaire universel, contenant generalement tous les mots françois tant vieux que modernes, et les termes de toutes les sciences et des arts.* Vol. 2. The Hague, 1690.

Helas je l'ay perdue. Paris, Bibliothèque nationale, MS fonds fr. 12744-anc. suppl. fr. no. 169; song no. 108.

Hotteterre, Jacques dit le Romain. *Airs et brunettes a deux et trois dessus pour les flutes traversieres tirez des meilleurs autheurs, anciens et modernes ensemble les airs de Mrs. Lambert, Lully, De Bousset, etc les plus convenables a la flute traversiere seule, ornez d'agrements par Mr. Hotteterre le Romain.* Paris, c. 1723. Facsimile reprint, Ann Arbor, Mich.: Early Music Facsimiles, n.d. The ornamented, unaccompanied pieces edited by David Lasocki as *Jacques Hotteterre le Romain Ornamented Airs and Brunettes,* London: Nova Music, 1980.

————. *L'Art de préluder sur la flute traversière, sur la flute-à-bec, sur le haubois, et autres instruments de dessus.* Paris, 1719. Edited by Michel Sanvoisin with resetting of type, Paris: Zurfluh, 1966.

————. *Principes de la flute traversiere, ou flute d'Allemagne, de la flute a bec ou flute douce, et du haut-bois devisez par traitez* (Paris, 1707). Facsimile of [1710] Amsterdam edition with German translation by H. J. Hellwig, Kassel: Bärenreiter, 1941. English translation by David Lasocki as *Principles of the Flute, Recorder, and Oboe,* London: Barrie & Rockliff; New York: Praeger, 1968. English translation by Paul Marshall Douglas as *Rudiments of the Flute, Recorder, and Oboe,* New York: Dover, 1968.

La Barre, Michel de. *Pièces pour la flûte traversière avec la basse continue.* Paris: Christophe Ballard, 1702.

Lainez, Alexandre. *Poësies de Lainez.* The Hague: Aux Dépens de la Compagnie, 1753.

Lalande, Michel-Richard de. *Symphonie des noëls* from *Recueil d'airs detachez et d'airs de violons* (1727). Bibliothèque nationale MS Vm^7 3077, 212–51. Modern edition edited by Rudolf Ewerhart as *Symphonie des Noëls für Melodieinstrumente (Blockflöten, Flöten, Oboen, Violinen) und Basso continuo* (3 vols.), Celle, Germany: Moeck, n.d.

Lebègue, Nicolas. *Troisieme livre d'orgue . . . et tous les noëls les plus connus . . . que l'on peut jouer sur l'orgue et le clavecin.* Paris, 1685. Edited by Norbert Dufourq as *Noëls variés,* Orgue et liturgie no. 16, Paris: Éditions musicales de la Schola cantorum et de la Procure générale de musique, 1952.

Le Blanc, Hubert. *Defense de la basse de viole contre les entreprises du violon et les prétentions du violoncel.* Amsterdam, 1740.

Le Moigne, Lucas. *S'Ensuivent plusieurs chansons de Noelz nouveau [sic] et speciallement les nouelz que composa feu Maistre Lucas le moigne en son vivant curé de sainct George du puys la garde au diocesze Poytou.* Paris, 1520. Chantilly, Musée Condé IV.C.40; Paris, Bibliothèque nationale, Rés. Ye 4315.

[*Livre de noëls*] (c. 1483–98). Paris, Bibliothèque nationale, MS fonds fr. 2368.

[Lotrian, Alain], publ. *Les grans nouelz nouveaux reduitz sur le chant de plusieurs chansons nouvelles tant en francoys, escossois, poitevin que limousin* (c. 1525–47). Paris, Bibliothèque nationale, Rés. Pet. Ye. 2684^1.

Le manuscrit dit des basses danses de la Bibliothèque de Bourgogne. Brussels, Bibliothèque royale, section des manuscrits, no. 9085. Facsimile reprint with introduction and transcription by Ernest Closson, Brussels: Société des bibliophiles et iconophiles de Belgique, 1912.

[Mareschal, Pierre, and Barnabé Choussard], publ. *Les nouelz faictz a l'onneur de Jhesuchrist. Et sont ordonnez coment on les doit chanter.* Lyons, c. 1504–6.

Mercure de France (Paris), 1 June 1725, 1081, and 11 December 1728, 2896–7.

Mersenne, Marin. *Traité des instruments,* the books on instruments from *Harmonie universelle, contenant la théorie et la pratique de la musique.* Paris: Sebastien Cramoisy, 1636. Facsimile reprint, edited by François Lesure (3 vols.), vol. 3, Paris: Editions du Centre National de la Recherche Scientifique, 1963. The books on instruments translated by Roger E. Chapman as *Harmonie Universelle: The Books on Instruments*, The Hague: Martinus Nijhoff, 1957.

[Moderne, Jaques], publ. *La fleur des noelz nouvellement notés en choses faictes imprimez en l'honeur de la nativité de nostre seigneur Jesuchrist et de la tressacrée mere.* Lyon, [1535]. Seville, Biblioteca Colombina 15.2.16.

_____. *S'Ensuyvent plusieurs basses dances.* N.p., n.d.

Montéclair, Michel Pignolet de. *Brunetes anciènes et modernes apropriées à la flûte traversière avec une basse d'accompagnement, premier recüeil.* Paris, c. 1721–33. British Library C. 23. SCH:1108.

Noëls (c. 1674). Paris, Bibliothèque de l'Arsenal, MS 3176.

Olivier, Gervais. *Cantiques de noelz anciens les mieux faicts et les plus requis du commun peuple: composez par plusieurs anciens autheurs a l'honneur de la nativité de nostre sauveur Jesus-Christ et de la vierge Marie.* Le Mans: Françoys Olivier, c. 1600.

Oudot, Nicolas, publ. *La grande bible des noels tant viels que nouveaux.* Troyes and Paris, 1684 and 1727.

Pasquier, Estienne. *Les recherches de la France.* Paris: Laurens Sonnius, 1571. Reprint, reviewed, corrected, and reordered, Paris: Louys Billaine, 1665.

Pellegrin, [Abbé] Simon-Joseph. *Cantiques spirituels, sur les points les plus importans de la religion, de la morale chrétienne, et sur lez quinze mysteres du rosaire; accompagnez d'hymnes pour les principales fêtes de l'année, et à l'honneur de tous les saints. Sur des airs d'opera, vaudevilles choisis, sur les chants de l'eglise, et des noëls anciens, notez, pour en faciliter le chant.* Paris: Nicolas Le Clerc, 1728.

_____. *Chants des noëls anciens.* Paris, Nicolas Le Clerc, 1718.

_____. *Noëls nouveaux pour l'année sainte, sur les chants de l'eglise, des anciens airs d'opera, de noels très-connus, et vaudevilles choisis, notez pour en faciliter le chant.* Nouvelle ed., revûë, et corrigée. Second recueil. Paris: Nicolas Le Clerc, 1732. [1st ed., 1701.]

_____. *Noëls nouveaux pour l'année sainte, sur les chants des noels anciens, et chansons spirituelles pour tout le cours de l'année, sur des airs d'opera et vaudevilles tres-connus.* 2nd ed., revûë, et corrigée. Premier recueil. Paris: Nicolas Le Clerc, 1715. [1st ed., 1701.]

_____. *Noëls nouveaux sur les chants des noels anciens, et chansons spirituelles pour tout le cours de l'année. Sur des airs d'opera et vaudevilles tres-connus, notez pour en faciliter le chant.* 2nd ed., revûë, et corrigée. Paris: Nicolas Le Clerc, 1702. [1st ed., 1701.]

_____. *Noëls nouveaux sur les chants des noels anciens. Notez pour en faciliter le chant.* 2nd ed., revûë, et corrigée. Paris: Nicolas Le Clerc, 1735. [1st ed., 1701.]

Rabelais, François. *Le cinquième et dernier livre des faicts et dits héroïques du bon Pantagruel.* In *Œuvres complètes,* edited by Guy Demerson. Paris: Editions du Seuil, 1973.

Raguenet, François. *Paralele des italiens et des françois en ce qui regarde la musique et les opéra.* Brussels, 1702. Facsimile reprint, Geneva: Minkoff, 1976.

Raison, André. *Second livre d'orgue. . . . L'Auteur adjoûte plusieurs noels propres pour des recits, et offertes au natural, et transposé, avec plusieurs variations dans le goût du temps, tant pour l'orgue, que pour le clavecin.* Paris, [1714]. Edited by Gaston Litaize and Jean Bonfils as *Second livre d'orgue* (2 vols.), L'Organiste Liturgique nos. 39–40 and nos. 43–4, Paris: Editions musicales de la Schola cantorum et de la Procure générale de musique, 1963.

Recueil de vieulx et nouveaulx noels recueillez par Frer Jehan de Vilgontier, prebstre, religieux profès de l'Abbaye de la Coulture, Prieur de Saint Saulveur, pres Fresnay (c. 1595). Paris, Bibliothèque nationale, MS fonds fr. 14983 [the Vilgontier MS].

Rippert, [Jean-Jacques?]. *Brunettes ou petits airs a II dessus, a l'usage de ceux qui veulent appendre à joüer de la flûte-traversiere. Avec une tablature de cet instrument.* Paris: Vve. Boivin, Le Clerc, 1725. *Recueil de noëls* and *Premier recueil de brunettes* edited by Roger Bernolin as *Jean-Jacques Rippert: Premier recueil de noëls et brunettes a deux dessus,* Paris: Alphonse Leduc, 1980.

Rousseau, Jean-Jacques. *Dictionnaire de musique.* Paris, 1768. Facsimile reprint, N.Y.: Johnson Reprint Corporation, 1969.

Sergent, Pierre, publ. *Les grans noelz nouveaulx composez nouvellement en plusieurs langaiges sur le chant de plusieurs belles chansons nouvelles.* Paris, [1537?]. Wolfenbüttel, Herzog August Bibliothek, Lm Smlbd. 54[1] [microfilm].

Tisserand, Jehan. *S'Ensuyt une tres belle salutation faicte sur les sept festes de Nostre-Dame laquelle l'on chante au salut à Sainct Innocent à Paris. Et la fit et composa frère Jehan Tissarant.* After 1519. Paris, Bibliothèque nationale, Rés. p. Ye. 301.

[Toulouze, Michel], publ. *L'Art et instruction de bien dancer.* Paris, [1488?]. Facsimile reprint with bibliographical note by Victor Scholderer, London: The Royal College of Physicians of London, 1936.

Tournes, Jan de. *Noelz vieux et nouveaux en l'honneur de la nativité Jesus Christ, et de sa tresdigne mere.* Lyon, 1557.

[Trepperel, Jean, Vve. de?]. *Les grans noelz nouveaulx fait a l'honneur et reverence de nostre saulveur Jesuchrist et de sa doulce mere.* Paris, c. 1515.

19TH AND 20TH CENTURIES

Anderies, John. "Chansons, Airs & Brunettes: The Practice of Playing French Vocal Music on the Transverse Flute." Transcript of Masters degree lecture-recital, Case Western Reserve University, 1993.

_____. "Vocal Music for the Transverse Flute." *Traverso* 6, no. 3 (July 1994): 1–3.

Arma, Paul. *Noël! Chantons Noël!* Paris: Les Editions Ouvrières, 1942.

Babelon, Jean. "*La fleur des noels* [Lyon, 1535]." *Revue des livres anciens* 1 (1913–14): 369–404.

Bachelin, Henri. *Les noels français.* Paris: Editions Musicales de la Librairie de France, 1927.

Backman, E. Louis. *Religious Dances in the Christian Church and in Popular Medicine.* Westport, Conn.: Greenwood Press Publishers, 1952. Reprint, 1977.

Barbazan, Etienne, ed. *Fabliaux et contes des poètes françois des XI, XII, XIII, XIV, et XVe siécles,* revised by M. Méon. Vol. 2. Paris: Crapelet, 1808.

Bladé, J.-F. *Poésies populaires de la Gascogne.* 3 vols. Paris, 1881.

Block, Adrienne Fried. *The Early French Parody Noël.* 2 vols. Studies in Musicology, ed. George Buelow, no. 36. Ann Arbor, Mich.: UMI Research Press, 1983 [revision of Ph.D. dissertation (City University of New York, 1979, copyright 1978)].

Bowers, Jane M. "'Flaüste traverseinne' and 'Flûte d'Allemagne': The Flute in France from the Late Middle Ages up through 1702." *Recherches sur la musique française classique* 19 (1979): 7–50.

_____. "French Flute School from 1700 to 1760." Ph.D. diss., University of California, Berkeley, 1971.

_____. "New Light on the Development of the Transverse Flute between about 1650 and about 1770." *Journal of the American Musical Instrument Society* 3 (1977): 5–56.

Brown, Howard Mayer. *Music in the French Secular Theater, 1400–1550.* Cambridge, Mass.: Harvard University Press, 1963.

Cammaert, Gustave. "Les brunettes." *Revue belge de musicologie* 11, fasc. 1–2 (1957): 35–51.

Canteloube, Joseph, ed. "Quand Dieu naquit à Noël!" Paris: Heugel et Cie., 1952.

Dobbins, Frank. "Noël." *The New Grove Dictionary of Music and Musicians,* 1980.

Eastwood, Tony. "The French Air in the Eighteenth Century: A Neglected Area." *Studies in Music* (University of Western Australia, Nedlands) no. 18 (1984): 84–107.

Gastoué, Amédée. *Le cantique populaire en France.* Lyon: Janin Frères, 1924.

_____. *Noëls anciens.* 4 vols. Paris, 1909 (vols. 1–2), 1922 (vols. 3–4).

Grimes, Conrad. "The Noels of Louis-Claude Daquin." *The Diapason* 60, no. 1 (1968): 24–7.

Guenther, Eileen Morris. "Composers of French Noël Variations in the 17th and 18th Centuries." Parts 1–3. *The Diapason* 65, no. 1 (1973): 1–5; 65, no. 2 (1974): 1–4; 65, no. 3 (1974): 4–5, 13.

Heartz, Daniel. "Mary Magdalen, Lutenist." *Journal of the Lute Society of America* 5 (1972): 52–67.

_____. "*Au pres de vous.* Claudin's Chanson and the Commerce of Publishers' Arrangements." *Journal of the American Musicological Society* 24 (1971): 193–225.

_____. "The Basse Dance: Its Evolution circa 1450 to 1550." *Annales Musicologiques* (Neuilly-sur-Seine: Société de Musique d'Autrefois) 6 (1958–63): 287–340.

_____. "Basse Dance." *The New Grove Dictionary of Music and Musicians,* 1980.

_____. "Branle." *The New Grove Dictionary of Music and Musicians,* 1980.

_____. "Mary Magdalen, Lutenist." *Journal of the Lute Society of America* 5 (1972): 52–67.

Heldt, Elizabeth. *Französiche Virelais aus dem 15. Jahrhundert.* Halle, 1916.

Hugon, Roger, Brigitte François-Sappey, and Norbert Dufourcq. "Le livre de noëls de Pierre Dandrieu, une énigme? Trois points de vue." *Recherches sur la musique française classique* 19 (1979): 102–94.

Huguet, Edmond. *Dictionnaire de la langue française du seizième siècle.* Paris, Didier, 1946, vols. 1–7.

Huizinga, Johan. *The Waning of the Middle Ages.* Garden City, 1954.

Jackman, James L. *Fifteenth Century Basse Dances: Brussels Bibl. Roy. MS. 9085 Collated with Michel Toulouze's* L'Art et instruction de bien dancer. Wellesley, Mass.: Wellesley College, 1964.

Lasocki, David, ed. *Fluting and Dancing: Articles and Reminiscences for Betty Bang Mather on Her 65th Birthday.* New York: McGinnis & Marx, 1988.

Lemeignen, Henri. *Vieux noëls composés en l'honneur de la naissance de Notre-Seigneur Jésus-Christ.* 3 vols. Nantes, 1876.

Lesure, François. "Danses et chansons à danser au début du XVIe siècle." In *Recueil de travaux offert à M. Clovis Brunel,* 176–84. Paris, 1955.

Little, Meredith Ellis, and Suzanne G. Cusick. "Allemande," *The New Grove Dictionary of Music and Musicians,* 1980.

Littré, Emile. *Dictionnaire de la langue française.* Vol. 5. Colombes: Gallimard et Hacette, 1957.

Marcel, Pierre. *La peinture française au début du dix-huitième siècle.* Paris, 1906.

Margolin, Jean-Claude. *Erasme et la musique.* Paris, 1965.

Mather, Betty Bang. *Interpretation of French Music from 1675 to 1775 for Woodwind and Other Performers.* New York: McGinnis & Marx, 1973.

Mather, Betty Bang, and David Lasocki. *Free Ornamentation in Woodwind Music: 1700–1775.* New York: McGinnis & Marx, 1976.

Mather, Betty Bang, with the assistance of Dean M. Karns. *Dance Rhythms of the French Baroque.* Bloomington: Indiana University Press, 1988.

Meylan, Raymond. *La Flûte.* Lausanne: Payot, 1974. German translation by Ilse Krämer and Raymond Meylan as *Die Flöte.* Bern and Stuttgart: Hallwag Verlag, 1974. English translation by Alfred Clayton as *The Flute.* Portland, Oregon: Amadeus Press, 1988.

Myrand, Ernest. *Noëls anciens de la nouvelle-France.* 2nd ed. Quebec: Typ. Laflamme & Proulx, 1907.

Neumann, Frederick. *Ornamentation in Baroque and Post-Baroque Music.* Princeton: Princeton University Press, 1978.

The New Grove Dictionary of Music and Musicians. Edited by Stanley Sadie. 20 vols. London: Macmillan; Washington, D.C.: Grove's Dictionaries of Music, 1980.

Pineau, Joseph. *Le mouvement rhythmique en français: principes et méthode d'analyse.* Paris: Klincksieck, 1979.

Poole, Elissa. "The *Brunetes* and Their Sources: A Study of the Transition from Modality to Tonality in France." *Recherches sur la musique française classique* 25 (1987): 187–206.

_____. "The Sources for Christophe Ballard's *Brunetes ou petits airs tendres* and the Tradition of Seventeenth-Century French Song." Ph.D. diss., University of Victoria, 1985.

Poulaille, Henry, ed. *La fleur des chansons d'amour de XVIe siècle.* Paris: Éditions Bernard Grasset, 1943.

_____. *La grande et belle bible des noëls anciens.* 3 vols. Paris: Editions Albin Michel, 1942 (vol. 1), 1950 (vol. 2), 1951 (vol. 3).

Rahn, Douglas J. "Melodic and Textual Types in French Monophonic Song ca. 1500." Ph.D. diss., Columbia University, 1978.

Ranum, Patricia M. "Les 'caractères' des danses françaises." *Recherches sur la musique française classique* 23 (1985): 45–70.

_____. "Do French Dance Songs Obey the Rules of Rhetoric?" In *Fluting and Dancing: Articles and Reminiscences for Betty Bang Mather on her 65th Birthday,* edited by David Lasocki, 104–30. New York: McGinnis & Marx, 1988.

_____. "A Fresh Look at French Wind Articulations," *American Recorder,* December 1992.

_____. "*Tu-Ru-Tu* and *Tu-Ru-Tu-Tu*: Toward an Understanding of Hotteterre's Tonguing Syllables." *The Recorder in the 17th Century: Proceedings of the International Recorder Symposium Utrecht 1993*, ed. David Lasocki. Utrecht: STIMU [Stichting voor Muziekhistorische Uitvoeringspraktijk], 1996.

Reese, Gustav. *Music in the Renaissance*. Rev. ed. New York and London: W. W. Norton, 1959.

Sahlin, Margit. *Etude sur la carole médiévale*. Uppsala: Almquist and Wiksells, 1940.

Saint-Arroman, Jean. *L'Interpretation de la musique française 1661–1789*. Paris: Librairie Honoré Champion, 1985.

Smidt, J. R. H. de. *Les noëls et la tradition populaire*. Amsterdam: H. J. Paris, 1932.

Tiersot, Julien. *Histoire de la chanson populaire en France*. Paris: E. Plon, Nourrit, 1889.

Wardropper, Bruce W. "The Religious Conversion of Profane Poetry." In *Studies in the Continental Background of Renaissance English Literature: Essays presented to John L. Lievsay*, edited by Dale B. J. Randall. Durham, N.C., 1977.

Waterhouse, William. *The New Langwill Index*. London: Tony Bingham, 1993.

Wilkins, Nigel. "Virelai." *The New Grove Dictionary of Music and Musicians*, 1980.

INDEX

An italicized numeral indicates an example, figure, or table; a bolded numeral, a choreography.

BETTY BANG MATHER is professor of flute at The University of Iowa. Her books include *Interpretation of French Music from 1675 to 1775*; *Dance Rhythms of the French Baroque*; and, with David Lasocki, *Free Ornamentation in Woodwind Music*, *The Classical Woodwind Cadenza*, and *The Art of Preluding*.

GAIL GAVIN graduated in 1995 from The University of Iowa, where she was a Presidential Scholar, an Undergraduate Scholar Assistant, and studied flute with Betty Bang Mather. In 1994 she received a Younger Scholar's Research Grant from the National Endowment for the Humanities.